FUNDRAISING FOR YOUTH

Hundreds of Wonderful Ways of Raising Funds for Youth Organizations

by
DORTHY M. ROSS

Illustrated by
BILL GRAY

Meriwether Publishing Ltd., Publisher
P.O. Box 7710
Colorado Springs, CO 80933

Editor: Arthur Zapel
Typography: Mary Rich and Kathy Pijanowski
Cover design: K. Anne Kircher
Inside design: Michelle Gallardo

Printed in the United States of America
First Edition.

The Library of Congress has cataloged the first printing of this title as follows:

Ross, Dorthy M.
Fundraising for youth : hundreds of wonderful ways of raising funds for youth organizations.--Colorado Springs, c1985.

242 p. : ill. ; 21 cm.

ISBN 0-916260-28-3 (pbk.)

1.Fund raising--United States. 2. Youth--United States--Societies and clubs.
I. Title.
HV41.R578 1985 369.4'068--dc19 84-61477
AACR 2 MARC

To Dana Ross, John and Heidi Mitchler, T. Henry Abel, William Baird, John Hauck and Dorothy Kramer, all Honorary Presidents of Illinois Society Children of the American Revolution, who let me share their world and all their fun; to all the other Super Kids of I.S.C.A.R. who turned Compass Point Farm into TETOF just by showing up; to Peter and Francie Ann, for helping load, unload and carry all the flags, books, boxes, T-shirts and other necessary junk; and to North, who kept the home fires burning and never complained when the rest of us drove off in the Ford to C.A.R.e FOR AMERICA!

TABLE OF CONTENTS

1 Why This Book?

Why This Book?

No matter what the economy, if you belong to a club or any type of organization, one of the first things you'll hear brought up under New Business (and sometimes Old Business) is the need for raising funds.

Funds.

Sometimes a little, sometimes a lot. To keep the ball rolling. Or perhaps more realistically, to keep those Little League balls flying into the outfield. Or to outfit the football team. Or take underprivileged kids to a game. Or to put in a new bike path in the village park. Or maybe just enough to keep postage money available so the monthly meeting reminder cards can be mailed out. Or – whatever.

The funds can come from your pocket, your bank account, your savings account. Providing, of course, the funds are there in the first place. And here comes that old word again. Economy, THE economy.

Okay, times are tough, people are looking for work and there just isn't a lot of money flying around to keep all these good works flourishing. But we can't just give up, can we? The question, then, is HOW?

Raising funds for community activities can be relatively easy with just a bit of planning. More importantly, it can turn out to be lots of fun. And it can revive a flagging community spirit – just by planning and working TOGETHER.

The sight of that well-filled club coffer brimming over with pennies, nickels and dimes (not to mention dollars) to aid your community cause puts a lilt into the voice, a smile on the face, a skip in the step, and causes everyone involved to walk a little prouder.

And – it can be easy. I promise.

As parents of three grown (if you count a college freshman, our youngest, as grown) children, my husband and I have been involved in light-years of 4-H Clubs, Rainbow Girls, DeMolay Boys, Future Farmers, Future Homemakers, Future Secretaries, Science Club, Madrigal Club, Children of the American Revolution, and others – as well as our own adult organizations – all intent on raising funds for whatever cause they have selected.

At one time or another we've peddled everything but sin and our nation's national defense secrets. We've seen it done the hard way – and because we are (we admit) primarily both lazy and not too affluent, we've figured out some ways to do it the other way – the EASY way. Usually, if not always, the easy way is the FUN way.

Our kitchen and dining tables have been loaded with sales kits, tickets, posters, mailing lists, brochures, tee shirts and stationery of all sorts. The garage has been stacked with cartons of pecans, popcorn, candy, vanilla extract and pepper cans, as well as garage sale goodies. Our station wagon has traveled countless miles, turning in at each driveway along the street or road, pushing our special project. Cheese, paper napkins, pizzas, greeting cards, candy, popcorn. It wasn't always fun.

In this book we will discuss direct sales and some of the very reputable companies we have dealt with. We will go into some long-range types of projects which take a lot of time planning and require the help of all the family, from grandparents to the family dog, in getting it accomplished.

Mostly, however, we will show you how your ingenuity and the things you have around the homestead already, the people you know in your own organizations, and a little bit of planning and work can spin gold for the club kitty.

Yes, you'll have to do a little work, spend a little time, sweat a little bit, and get involved. You may even worry a bit, but our goal is to take as much of that from your shoulders as possible, using some of the secrets we've come across over the years. Most of them shouldn't be secrets anyhow, and because we believe in your good causes as we have our own (and will no doubt continue to do, although we've traded in the wagon for a smaller car), we want to share these ideas with you.

2 The Basic Basics

Choosing the Right Chairperson; Offering Choices; Personal Safety; Zoning & Ordinances; Using Your Resources; Security; Thank-yous

The Basic Basics

First of all, start with the premise that there is no sure-fire, guaranteed, easy, fun way to raise funds for your organization. But some ways are easier than others. Some are easier for some groups, some would be difficult or impossible for a particular group, and it's up to you to choose the best one for your situation.

The next thing that is involved is PLANNING.

Regardless of the route you choose to go, all sorts of details will have to be worked out carefully, which means you must know the details before you can work them out. You must also know how much time and effort you and others are willing to spend to bring about the end result – money in your club treasury.

The chairperson you select for your project is probably your most important decision. He or she may be a dynamic, take-charge person, but if the taking-charge results in hurt feelings, broken promises and a total or even partial breakdown of communications within your organization or community, you still lose. Your chairman must be reliable, energetic, interested in the specific cause, and able to get along with those who will be working alongside, if your fundraiser is to be successful.

Because this book is aimed primarily at those of you who are working with youth organizations, remember they can take on some fairly complicated or long-lasting chores IF they have adults working alongside or in the background.

If you're a youth organization senior leader, you have probably already figured out that the five letters which spell out "youth" or "young" start with three others — Y–O–U. You, the parent; you, the adult. Adult leaders are an essential part of any youth organization, and if you're the parent of that nine-year-old just now earning the small bronze 4-H Club pin for first year membership, you've got a long way to go. You'll be knee-deep in fund drives until your youngest is completed with Scouts, 4-H, church youth groups, or whatever. Hopefully this book will make those years easier – and lots more fun.

Another thing we think it important to point out is that as a youth leader, one of the most important things you can remember to assure success in their projects is to GIVE THE KIDS A CHOICE when you're passing out things like work. If you, the adult, decide what project they will do, how they will do it, and then proceed to give them orders, just like the miniature adults they are, they will rebel. Let them decide which project (you offer the options) they will undertake, and then give them their choice on which chores they will do, after the understanding has been reached that some of the chores will be less glamorous than others, that being the name of the game.

The choice may be, at your own home, which pair of oldish jeans they can wear to work on "Rent-A-Kid Day" or the actual chore they will be assigned, whether washing windows, raking the lawn, or scrubbing that floor. You'll find there is little or no resentment over the hard work they're going to be putting in if they are given a choice between the various jobs. You'll be treating them in an adult, mature manner, and they'll return the favor by acting in adult, mature ways. It's like telling bored kids to "go play" instead of saying, "Do you want to play ball, get out the Monopoly game, or set up the card table for a jigsaw puzzle?" Give them a choice – this is, after all, their group you're raising funds for.

Another basic – and perhaps the most important in this book – is to remember if you're sending your kids into the homes (or businesses) of people with whom you are not well acquainted, you may want to accompany them if they are of a particularly young age group, have them make regular phone check-back calls with a central monitor or any other means of assuring their personal safety. Money can be printed on presses but kids can't, so their safety is paramount, no matter how important your cause!

The next step is selecting the date for your event. If you need another event to help draw a crowd for your sales effort, by all means hitch your wagon to such an event, making certain, of course, that you are not in conflict or competition with the event itself. As an example, if the Art Association is sponsoring an art show, your nearby refreshment stand would benefit from the crowd drawn by the art displays.

On the other hand, it would not be in the best interest of the group or the community to set up your own Pepsi booth next to the Coke booth they're having at the ballgame, regardless of all the taste-testing advertising you may have seen on TV. You must remember that a successful fundraiser shares a spirit of mutual community concerns. If your venture stirs up dissension among another competing groups, you will have lost ground before you even set up your little booth.

If you feel your venture can stand on its own feet, be sure to steer away from conflicting dates of other events. A benefit donkey basketball game in one school gym should not have to compete with a celebrity basketball game across town in the other school gym. And it plays heck with that old community spirit.

If your event is an outdoor affair, plan a rain date, just in case. Unless your effort directly ties in with a holiday, it may be best to steer away from those dates, because your best customers – as well as your best helpers – will be taking off for a weekend trip to Grandma's, the lake, or. . .

With the exception of holiday weekends, probably THE best times to hold your fundraiser are Saturdays, Sundays and Friday evenings which lead into a weekend event.

You can't do too much planning nor too much making of lists. Plan carefully, make lists and checklists. At your first meeting after you've decided what you're going to DO for your fundraiser, have everyone make their own lists and then make a composite of all those lists. What you've forgotten very likely someone else will have thought of.

You need to think about budget, equipment, advertising, patron support, time elements for each stage of your production, what resources you already have, what you can beg, borrow or rent, the legal aspects of what you're doing, and how each step will be accomplished.

You should have a goal. If you know what the uniforms for the team will cost it's easy to arrive at the amount of your goal. If you are just operating under the assumption of putting money into the club treasury to be spent at a future time for a future need, it is more important to weigh that sum against the amount of money which will be used to raise X amount of dollars. You're wasting everyone's time and money if you spend $100 to make $50, so it's important to have a goal in the first place and to be sure you've selected a viable project to raise the needed or desired funds.

If you reside in a large urban area with lots of zoning restrictions you need to check with your municipal officials to make sure what you are planning will not break any laws or ordinances. Even if you're a rural or small town organization it's good to check with your local officials as to location, date, and the brief description of your project. Often they can give you valuable information which will make your work a lot easier. They know, for instance, about the traffic flow on the various streets and roads and can advise you as to whether you may need traffic wardens where your customers will be driving onto the property where your project will be held (which is often a necessity during 'rush' hours, such as those hours when commuters will be going to or getting home from work, and at the opening and closing of your project). Your customers' safety is at stake, not to mention the young people and their families who will be running the show.

Depending on the type of organization you represent there may be taxes involved in your venture. Non-profit groups often are exempt from income tax payment (unless they make an awful lot of money) but are required to pay certain other taxes such as sales or amusement taxes or other levies. You may be required to purchase a local permit of some sort in order to put on your event.

If you are selling a product or a service from another person or firm, you may need a contract. Here is an excellent example of using your neighborhood resources – if one of your member's father is an attorney, enlist his aid. He may be more than willing to donate his advice even though his calendar doesn't give him time to come the day of the big event and add his muscle power. He has a special resource; use it. You want everything to be legal and safe; you want to be sure you're not led down the proverbial garden path by someone who wants you to sign their contract. If you've ordered items for sale on a certain date make sure your contract guarantees delivery by that date in a salable condition (meaning A-1, super-duper, perfect condition). You can't very well deliver Christmas greenery, for example, if it isn't delivered until December 26th.

So, no matter how good that salesman's pitch sounds, beware – and utilize your attorney friend. Don't sign a paper which requires you to pay for more stuff than can be quickly sold in your community. Be aware of the headcount your members will be reaching in their sales efforts: sixteen members can reach a lot of customers, but only SO many. The salesman makes a larger commission on selling you a large quantity. Make sure you're going for quality. The quantity you sell will increase as a result and you'll have set a precedent for next year's sales. (Remember – we said you had a long way to go – at least until your youngest 'graduates' from all this nonsense!)

Back to our lawyer-father-friend. If you're offering the public anything like a commercial carnival with rides and games, it is not just important, but vital, that the firms and operators be reputable, that their rides be safe, and that they carry their own liability insurance – in large enough amounts. A lawyer can look over any papers you're required to sign and is probably more familiar with local ordinances which may affect your sales effort. Again, don't be afraid to ask him for free legal advice. If he's a mere acquaintance as opposed to a family member, he is able to deduct free advice to your group from his income tax if he wishes. It's also a good learning process for your members to sit in on some of the legal conferences and it will give them valuable information which will come in handy in class and in later years.

Take advantage of the insurance-expert-father in your group (don't overlook the insurance-expert-mother, either!). It may be that you should carry some special liability coverage of your own. You don't have to buy from that individual unless you want to, but you do need some advice, and buying your one-day policy (or whatever you decide is necessary) from your advisor would be a way of saying thank you.

There is also the possibility you may need some sort of security during your event. Discuss it with your local police officials and get their advice. Take the members along with you on this trip, too

– another excellent learning opportunity. Some of the things which might come up at your function could be lost children, shoplifting, or unruly persons causing a disturbance. If there will be a lot of action where persons could be injured, you must have a nurse handy at all times. Even at a small, quiet event it's well to have a nurse around and, again, you can likely find a nurse within the ranks of your group/family. Don't be afraid to ask. They could man a first-aid stand where it might not be at all 'their thing' to sell peanuts in the gallery.

Decide who will be in charge of publicity. Who will construct your booths. Who will haul in supplies – carry out the trash – count the money – haul it to the bank.

And – VERY IMPORTANT – save your lists. They'll probably need to be recopied, but do save them, and help make next year's fundraiser that much easier. Those lists represent the blueprint for next year's successful project.

Another thing we think is important is to take time to thank those who helped you – and especially those outside your organization. A short card, or a visit, just to say 'thanks'. The attorney for his free advice, the police captain who assured you someone from his staff would be nearby in case of an emergency, the nurse who got her white uniform out of the back of the closet to be handy – just in case. There's always next year, and just as you wish to pay all your cash bills for expenses for your project, you want to make sure all your other debts of gratitude are paid too. Community spirit, remember? Not to mention common courtesy.

We believe it is very important to KNOW YOUR AUDIENCE. It is important that you select a program which your members, with the probable help of their families, can carry out. It's also important that the project be one which will appeal to those in your neighborhood you depend on for your customers.

As an example, a group of boys is not going to put their heart and soul (not to mention their sweat) into a project which requires them to sell ultrafeminine stationery. There are only so many mothers, grandmothers and girlfriends they would approach for a sale, and they wouldn't dare go next door with their boxes of pink scented papers if their high school football hero might happen to answer the doorbell. Neither will you have much luck having a Pet Wash in a neighborhood where zoning prohibits pets.

Other examples of knowing your audience would be trying to sell boxes of candy in a neighborhood packed with dentists and their families, or popcorn to a neighborhood rich with older citizens who park their pearly whites in cups of water at night, or canned hams for Hanukkah celebrations. These may seem rather impious, facetious examples but I think you get the picture. One more warning – don't go for a candy sale in the summer months unless you like tons of melted chocolate getting in the tire treads when you drive into the garage after the sale is over. (Thank God it's over!)

Another aspect of knowing your audience is, again, to know the resources within your group. Don't send a shy, reticent member to sell tickets door to door. You won't redo your shy member and neither will you sell many tickets. Just as you wouldn't give the football halfback the job of ushering people to their seats while the 130-pound weakling member sets up the bleachers, try to spread your tasks according to the strongest talents of your members. And don't forget, try to give them an option – a choice of which job or chore. They need to make a few decisions of their own – another learning process. Besides, the more they learn, the sooner they get this leadership position and you can retire to the sidelines. Now, doesn't that sound just like heaven?

3 Breaking Budget Barriers

Use of Free Publicity Outlets; Media Magic; Smokey Bear and Woodsy Owl; Recycled Posters; Department Store Display Items; Saving Printers' Costs; How to Make Your Own Tickets With Stubs; Lists

Breaking Budget Barriers

How do you spend money you don't have in order to raise money for your group? Just as we have budget problems at home, so they loom on the very near horizon of the organization which wishes to make money for its project.

There are two methods. The first requires the participants to reach into their own pockets to pay for all the advance expenses of the program (or depend on their credit at the local merchants which is also dependent upon the individual member).

Or – you can make do with what you have.

For example – PUBLICITY. That's in capital letters because it's a VERY important part of your program. Start early with publicity, using all the resources at hand. Radio and television stations, for instance, are required by federal law to give so much free air time to causes of community concern. Contact the Community Affairs officer of each of your local radio and television stations and let them do your work for you. They know the most effective ways, too, so take advantage of their expertise.

It's expensive – very expensive – to buy publicity so figure out how you can get it without shelling out those badly needed dollars. Stage a 'pre' event, invite the media, have press releases available for distribution, and again, the media will do your work for you. Free.

You can't just call them up, though, and say, "We're going to announce our annual style show. Come and give us publicity." You have to convince them you have something to give them in return. And what they are looking for is NEWS! Your news can be hammy or eccentric – use your imagination – to announce or promote your fundraiser. Or it can be dramatic as you relate where your funds will go. As for example, a project whose funds will go to help underprivileged children or other persons or places with special, dramatic needs. Make sure your announcement is an attention-getter. Remember that it has to have NEWS appeal. Otherwise you'll have a press meeting and nobody – nobody at all – will show up.

So, hie yourself to the radio and television stations after making an appointment to see the Community Affairs officer. Tell them what your organization is all about, what your goals are, and what you plan to do to raise money toward reaching that goal. Let the kids do most of the talking, if at all possible.

Not only is it often possible to get a spot announcement on the air touting your project, it may just be possible that you can inspire that media officer to send a camera man to watch your committees working on booths (or whatever) and to tell of other aspects of your group's activities. Go prepared when you go to the station. And I cannot stress enough the importance of calling ahead and making an appointment to see the right person.

If you have printed brochures or other material about your organization, take them along. If you've had other fundraisers and have pictures of the work in action, take them along. Be prepared to answer questions about the organization, its members, and the goal and project. Whether you're representing the Boy Scouts or another group, BE PREPARED!

You must sell that media person on you and your group before you'll be able to sell him on helping you promote the project itself with free publicity. The station has free time, yes, but there are many demands for it, and you have to be certain your request is sincere and that your presentation is unique enough to catch their attention and make them want to help your cause.

The person who makes this media contact can be found among your member/family resources. Choose him or her carefully, making certain you have selected someone who knows all about the organization and can field any questions which may be asked.

If you plan a press meeting with many members of the media in attendance, make sure it's a whiz-bang! Costumes, animals, and little kids are eye catchers. If you can line up Smokey the Bear to help promote the conservation aspect of your group's project (assuming of course it does work in conservation) do so. (Contact your local office of Forestry or the State Forester or the local office of the Department of Agriculture for Smokey the Bear or Woodsy Owl.) The attendance and participation of Smokey, Woodsy and other national 'stars' lend credibility to your organization. The same is true of any other celebrities who might be available. If you can line up a national baseball or football player (who just happens to be a relative or neighbor) do so. A word of caution: be sure (no matter how many home runs he's hit) your baseball star has a personal life which relates to the principles of your youth group. Some athletes are highly paid stars, but their after-hours antics are not exactly what we are trying to teach our children.

With or without media coverage you will probably want to promote your project on a personal level, right in your own community. This will mean things like posters. Posters should saturate your consumer area. They should be colorful and eye-catching so that a busy housewife headed into the grocery store with a long list to buy will stop and read the information on the poster. Your publicity committee chairman is a very important person. It's up to that committee to make certain everyone knows about your fundraiser. You can help by providing catchy ideas for posters, information as to where posters should be placed and similar help.

Any organization of any size at all is bound to have some talented person art-wise. Again, use your resources. Line them up to help with the posters, use their talents and their ideas. It's free and it helps spread the work around so everyone has a great feeling when the big event is over and the money is on the way to the bank.

Even if your publicity budget is nil you don't have to depend on word-of-mouth to spread the word about your upcoming event. If posterboard is too expensive, why not make a deal with all your local merchants to be responsible for removing outdated posters of other groups from the store bulletin boards and then use the reverse side of the poster for YOUR publicity.

Those same merchants are excellent sources of material for posters. They buy and print their own, and they receive countless advertising posters from the national firms they buy from. Ask the grocer to let you recycle those posters. Use the reverse side or cover the printed side(s) with plain wrapping paper. No plain wrapping paper? Don't even think it! Look in the drawer where you keep your gift wrapping paper. You probably purchased a package or so months ago (or even years) that you've never used and maybe never will because the original package contained a variety of designs – weddings, baby gifts, birthday gifts, etc. If you're like most of us, you'll find yourself using one type more than the others and now have seventeen different designs of anniversary gift paper.

So, unfold one sheet of that anniversary gift paper you can't possibly use for a century, judging from how they're already stockpiled. Look at the reverse side. Did you ever see such nice white paper? A quick pressing with an iron and you have a smooth sheet of white paper with which to slipcover the used posterboard from the store. Voilà! A new poster is born.

Need something really eye-catching? Go to your theatre manager and talk him out of the life-size posters of the stars of the movies he showed last week (you may have to go while the feature is running and get your bid in early). Who better to hold a small placard advertising your comedy show than a popular comedian? Let your imagination run rampant. That's advertising.

Photo stores have great material in their windows. Contact the manager and ask for their hand-me-downs. Most of it had to be shipped flat to the store so that means you can store it flat, too, under your bed, behind a dresser, or wherever, until you have an actual need for it.

Go to your department store display manager and ask him for discards. Provide each source with a 3" x 5" file card on which you have plainly typed or printed your name, address, phone number (where you can be reached days or evenings), and the group or groups you represent. Even with the reduced display budgets of most stores today this is a pot of gold. But make that personal contact. And here again you should call ahead of time to make an appointment with the proper store personnel. This will save time as you will avoid the store shuffle where you are sent from division to division because no one is really sure what you want. The telephone operator is trained to help you reach the office of the person you need to talk to – from there it's easy to make an appointment.

One group my husband and I worked with for many years (Children of the American Revolution) has had award-winning floats in our state fair parade. The budget for the float has never gone over $50, because we used discarded department store display items we received free or for a token payment. A three-foot-tall, three-dimensional star (actually three stars, one each in red, white and blue) was the highlight of one award-winning float. Our expenses? The stars cost $1 each. If we'd gone to an advertising firm to purchase them, I hesitate to even guess what they would have cost. Our group took advantage of a bargain – the department store paid full price.

Another item which can cost you money is the table or tables on which you display your items for sale. Obviously, you can rent them but there goes some of the profit before you've even sold your first homemade cake.

Every home has card tables in the closet. Use them in rows and cover them with sheets from your linen closet. If you need something sturdier, find those handy saw horses which most farmers and many home-crafters or carpenters use. Top them with long boards or flat doors and you have your table at little or no expense. If you are displaying heavy or bulky items it is imperative your table be sturdy enough so you won't be embarrassed by a table leg folding under. Or worse yet, your workers or customers won't be burned by hot grease or injured by heavy items spilling from a table which suddenly gave up the ghost and folded its spindly little legs in surrender and defeat.

Many organizations have bunting stored away in someone's attic or closet. See if you can borrow it to skirt your display tables. It's relatively inexpensive so perhaps you can even buy your own, knowing it will last for years for future booths or floats. Maybe you can even rent it to another group with a fundraiser next week and recoup some of your expenses or buy in partnership with other organizations. A reminder: if you purchase red, white and blue bunting you should remember that according to the Flag Code of the United States, the red goes at the bottom, the blue at the top. One year we draped our C.A.R. float with the blue at the bottom, mostly because it had rained the night before and we figured any splashes would show up less on the dark blue. It was a bit embarrassing to be told afterwards (by several individuals) that our patriotic, historical organization had used the patriotic bunting incorrectly!

If you find you have absolutely NO artistic talent in your group (although that's hard to believe!) for the neat lettering of your posters, use other people's hard work. Cut out bright letters from magazine ads or covers, use pictures from catalogs, or even actual three dimensional items which call attention to your cause. As an example, if you're going to be holding an aluminum recycling drive, your poster can feature a used soda can taped to the poster. You might want to use a non-aluminum one for the poster, just in case it gets lost before you get it recycled.

If you're having a newspaper drive, your poster can have a crumpled-up sheet of colorful paper in one corner as a graphic. If you're having a bake sale use a cupcake paper, or for a candy sale use wrappers from candybars. Use your imagination (where have you heard that before?) and USE YOUR RESOURCES! You might want to use plastic spoons or forks to advertise a food sale or dinner you're sponsoring – or even some beat-up silver from the Goodwill. Use what you have in appealing ways and you won't need to hire anyone to do your group's publicity.

If you require tickets for your project stay away from the printer. We have nothing against printers (some of our best friends and favorite cousins are printers), but unless you can afford them you can route that same money to your cause by making your own tickets.

Practically every organization has someone who has access to a copy machine. Or even a duplicator. Spend an hour typing up your tickets on one sheet of paper then copy them on whatever machinery is available. Your members all have scissors with which to cut them apart and staplers to put them into booklets if required.

You need tickets with stubs because you're giving door prizes or raffling off a prize? No sweat. Make your own.

You still don't have to pay for an expensive printing job just because you need a ticket with a stub. Do your tickets as suggested above – typed, copied on the copier you have available and THEN it's ready for the personal touch to provide that stub and torn-off portion. You're doubtful? You think the stubs won't tear off straight and you'll be left with half an address for the grand prize winner? Alright, Doubting Thomases and Thomasinas. Come with us and we'll show you how. All it takes is a trip to your sewing machine.

Sewing machine for tickets? That's right. Unthread the machine, put in a sharp needle and run your sheets of tickets through, stitching along the tear-line between stub and ticket portion. The unthreaded needle will provide a perfect perforation line for your tickets which can now be cut apart and the stub ends stapled into booklets for easy handling. You'll be able to stitch several sheets of tickets at a time. Take a few trial runs to find out how many and BE SURE the sheets of tickets are in perfect alignment as you do your stitching.

If it's absolutely necessary that your tickets all be numbered, your members can number them, which is a time-consuming, boring job. Or you can find someone whose office has a numbering stamp machine – the kind which leaves consecutive numbers each time you push the handle down.

Again, use the resources you have. Don't be afraid to ask a local businessman for his help, financially, or for the loan of his office equipment. If you receive his cooperation it's tax deductible to the firm. And the worst that can happen is that you receive a NO answer.

When you go to such a businessman, be sure you go in a manner which tells him or her that you are in business, too, and that your primary business at this time is to help raise funds for your worthwhile cause. Again, as with the media, be prepared. Be prepared to sell yourself and your cause, whenever necessary.

Back to budget essentials – make up a list – in fact, you'll have several lists before this event is successfully over. If several aspects are involved don't be afraid to have a separate list for each action, each cause, each problem. It's easier to scratch out the item as you finish the chore instead of having to add items the day everything is happening and you have forgotten to do something important.

Some of the items for which money may (or will have to be) available up front are merchandise, equipment for your booth, advertising, prizes, and other supplies. Your committee should estimate as closely as possible what each of the expenses will be. There should be an itemization also of where your front money will come from (members' pockets – meaning Daddy's – or the club's already-depleted treasury, or credit from local merchants, or where?). Ultimately you may have to make another list of what you absolutely can't afford to do simply because you don't have the funds in the first place. Just as you can't afford to pay retail for something and sell it on the wholesale market (although my farmer husband and his counterparts have been doing so for years), you can't afford to go overboard on any one item unless you have a backer. And, if you've a big, big backer who's willing to kick in a bundle, you don't need to have this fundraiser in the first place!

Another cardinal rule is STICK TO YOUR BUDGET – unless there is a darned good (meaning money-making) reason for going over.

Something that has to be budgeted very, very carefully is time. Your time, your members' time, and the time between NOW and the day of your big fundraising event.

Remember that you can't decide on a Monday night to have a big, successful fundraiser for your good cause the following Saturday. It takes time; it takes planning; it takes work. But it can also take the everyday worries of the world out of your mind because you've become so busy working out the most successful ways to have your fundraiser. Most fundraisers will take from two months to a year to organize well and succeed.

What it mostly takes, too, is determination.

4 There's a Long, Long Trail Awinding (and a Lot of WORK Ahead)

Bazaars (with recipes for hot mustard, herb vinegars, mink toy instructions); Style Shows; Stage Productions; Exhibition Sports Events; Carnivals and Fairs (recipes for real lemonade, ant farms, feeders and houses for birds); Instant Ancestors; Kissing Booths; and more

There's a Long, Long Trail Awinding (and a Lot of WORK Ahead)

"Work before play," the old saying goes. So I'm putting in my two cents (or so) right now about those fundraisers that take up a lot of time to carry out and a lot of work done up front.

Some of these ideas are bazaars, style shows, anything that's presented on a stage, and exhibition sports games such as tennis matches or pro-am (professional-amateur) golf tourneys. Others are carnivals where your members are doing all the doing, as opposed to letting other individuals or groups participate on their own behalf (which you'll read about further along).

1 So, we'll begin with BAZAARS.

By definition, a bazaar is a marketplace. That means your group has to come up with something to sell to your customers. Unless you're ordering in a lot of junk from a commercial vendor, you and your members have to come up with a lot of homemade, salable, eye-catching, good-smelling, tasty, useful or unique items for your customers. And if you want to make a lot of money from a lot of customers, it means an awful lot of all of the above.

Do you want to spend months making potholders? Do you have enough mothers and grandmothers willing to make pints of grape jelly, or dozens of cookies, or scores of towels to hang from kitchen cabinet knobs, etc?

Are your young members interested enough in making leather wallets to spend two hours after every weekly meeting making more leather wallets to sell at next year's bazaar? No matter how excited they are when you pull out the easy instructions, assemble all the neat-looking leather craft tools, and show them a sample of the finished project, their excitement is going to wane as the weeks go by and so is their productivity and their quality workmanship.

In other words, are you sure – really sure –you want to have a bazaar?

If you have enough quality merchandise, you can make tons of money, and many church kitchens attest to that fact. Some of the things you will have to plan for are the time and place; how many items (and how many varieties of items) you wish to offer for sale and at what prices; where the merchandise will come from (it should be 99 percent homemade – and 100 percent quality); decorations; a theme (if any); plus all the other things like publicity which have to be worked out for any project.

Once you've selected the date and place and set your publicity committee to work, you might select a theme. Many bazaars are held in the fall with an eye toward providing customers with homemade Christmas gifts. The decorations can be carried out in either a harvest or Christmas theme motif to set the stage for your sales.

2 Using a harvest theme, make sure you have some home-grown pumpkins and squashes donated to the cause. They can serve as decorations first, then be sold and picked up at the close of the sale. A shock of corn or a scarecrow at the door is certain to set

the theme for your customers, getting them into the harvest spirit even before they get out of their cars.

3 Sell decorations for Halloween parties or favors for trick-or-treaters if it's close enough to October 31. Early fall flowers in arrangements in rustic utensils go over well this time of year, as do dried floral arrangements. Some darling Halloween ghosts can be made from styrofoam balls (for the head) tied to a dowel (for the arms) over which white sheeting is draped. The ghosts are made so you can hang them from doorways or tree limbs where they flutter frighteningly in the slightest breeze. Some sale items perfect for the food table are pumpkin pies, breads and cookies, ceramic pumpkins and Halloween figurines and commercial paper napkins and stationery carrying out the fall theme. You can also include back-to-school items if your bazaar is held in September.

4 If your bazaar has a Christmas holiday theme, you should plan to have a real or imitation Christmas tree from which your homemade tree ornaments will hang for quick and easy sale. Even your youngest members can make tiny felt ornaments. One of these might be a red felt horse-head-shaped stocking into which is stuck a red and white peppermint stick. Ornaments can be made from thread spools, flash cubes, paper chains, and strings of popcorn and/or cranberries. (Keep these fresh in the refrigerator until the day of the sale and feed them to the birds after the real Christmas tree comes down.) Your imagination can run riot as long as your quality stays high. Don't try to sell shoddy-looking homemades. You won't, anyway, and someone's feelings will be hurt if his/her contribution is left to hang on the otherwise denuded green tree. If the items have to be simple because of the age and abilities of your members, keep them simple and good. Try dolls made of wooden clothespins – they make easy magic.

5 Obvious sellers for Christmas bazaars are candies, cookies and breads of all sorts. If your event occurs quite a while before December 25th, provide the kinds of goodies which can be kept in the freezer until later gift-giving and use at Christmas.

6 Christmas stockings of all sorts sell well – knitted, crocheted, embroidered, appliquéd, quilted, or just plain sewn with a fringe or with lace added. Stray from the stocking shape if you have adequate seamstresses. Make up "socks" resembling cowboy boots, high-topped tenny pumps, fishermen waders, Victorian high-topped shoes (for the Victorian gents, add spats), or any other kind of footwear you can think of.

7 Tree skirts to go around the Christmas tree are popular items. Imagination will give your seamstresses lots of leeway for design. Try a red felt circle with green ball fringe or cut up that old torn quilt you inherited from your mother-in-law. Be sure to cut the skirt large enough to cover the tree stand.

8 Wreaths made from grapevines, corn shucks, straw, plastic greenery, braided cloth, yarns and what-have-you are good sellers. Start early with the grapevines. They have to be wet and tied into wreath shape. As we said before, you can't do a bazaar overnight.

9 Some really unique items for your bazaar can include small quantities of special recipes such as hot mustard. Our recipe for the hottest mustard you'll ever eat (it'll absolutely take the top of your head off) is made by adding flat beer (let it sit out uncovered for several hours to take out the fizz) to plain old dry mustard. Yes, the yellow powder that comes in the small tin cans on the spice shelf at the store. Add enough beer to give the powder the spreading consistency of regu-

lar mustard, put it into small containers (such as baby food jars) and add a warning: THIS STUFF IS HOT! (Softies can thin its potency down with regular salad mustard from the refrigerator – the kind you buy for hot dogs.)

10 Another good seller is herb vinegars. These should be made at least three weeks in advance of your bazaar and should be sold in pretty little bottles, cruets or decanters. Use an individual herb such as tarragon or mix several herbs such as dill and chives with parsley or rosemary, thyme with parsley, or chives with tarragon. Use commercial cider or white vinegar and fresh herbs. The recipe is simple: one quart of vinegar requires three tablespoons of herbs. Don't shatter the herb. Curl the sprig into a tablespoon to get the right measure (after washing all the herbs, of course) and then place the proper amount of herb into a sterile quart jar. Meanwhile, bring the vinegar to a boil in a pan and pour the hot vinegar into the jar up to an inch and a half from the top. (Use a funnel so you won't spill any – it's hot.) Put the cap (or cork, if using a large bottle) on and let it steep for at least three weeks. It will steep well if left in the sun on a window ledge or somewhere else outside where it won't get knocked over by a passing pet. Put the vinegar into smaller jars and bottles for sale, stick on a pretty label and ribbon, and you have a sure seller.

11 You can also make up small jars of herbs to sell as medicinal teas. (The small jars can be baby food jars which should never be thrown away if you have a hobbyist, bazaar or craft-minded person in the family or neighborhood – they come in too handy.) With pretty painted lids, stick-on labels and a ribbon necktie, you can sell lots of these herbs. The directions to accompany each should tell the purchaser to use about two teaspoons of a fresh herb (or one teaspoon of dried herb), add boiling water and let steep in the cup for several minutes. Strain, if desired. Use proportionately more in teapot. Some suggestions are: Chamomile flowers (for upset stomach, insomnia, headaches, lots more); Tansy (for colds – best to use young growth of this herb); Spearmint (a stimulant); Basil (for upset stomachs, also a stimulant); Lemon Balm (for headaches); Beebalm or Bergamont (for colds); Rosemary (for colds and headaches); Sage (for colds, headaches, stimulant); Lavender (for upset stomach and tension headaches) and many others. You can also make up little bags of herbs for teas, using such herbs as thyme, oregano and rosemary; lemon-scented geranium and mint (and sometimes thyme); rose-scented geranium and lemon thyme or lemon geranium; myrtle and thyme; and others. The recipe for serving: pour boiling water into a cup into which you've placed an ordinary tea bag and any of the above (slightly crushed fresh herbs). Leave herbs in cup while you sip. For summer cool drinks, use mint, peppermint, apple geranium; thyme, geranium, balm, verbena or any of the lemon-flavored herbs.

12 The pièce de résistance is – are you sitting down? – a mink teddy bear! You may never have seen such a pet on shelves of the toy store. In fact, I'll bet you haven't. But if you have a seamstress or two who is willing to make toys, and if you run across a cheap, damaged mink (you can use other furs) jacket, stole or coat in someone's closet or even find one for a small price at the Goodwill outlet, you can offer a boutique item to out-tique almost anything you've

ever seen. These can also be made on a 'by-order' basis, depending on the supply of available mink.

Use a regular toy teddy bear pattern from the fabric store. When sewing with leather or fur, you should remember to use the special leather needle (it's flat-sided as opposed to round). Also remember to apply white glue inside your seams before stuffing, to help strengthen your stitches. Grandmothers might love this project. It is pretty much a hand-stitching project although some of the longer seams could be done by sewing machine, again using the special leather or cutting needle available at the fabric or sewing machine stores. Add glass eyes (from the craft shop) and a pretty ribbon, and you have a very, very expensive (and moneymaking) item to offer your customers.

Obviously, you can make mink toys using other animal patterns – cats, lambs, etc. If the fur you have is stiff (the leather backing), or the individual hairs are falling out, don't waste your time trying to salvage it because it won't look good enough to sell, anyway. You can often use several different colors or kinds of left-over furs if you use your imagination and want to come up with something really different. Don't offer this project to a grandmother who's allergic to animals. There will be flying furry stuff in the vicinity of the sewing project. (If anything else flies out of the old furs throw the whole thing in the fireplace, light a match and forget the entire thing!)

13 With a bazaar (as with most projects), you should make a floor plan of the area where it will be held. Allocate your space according to the potential each booth offers financially. No matter how much your member complains, you can't give more space to the dollar kites than you do to the five dollar boutique tree ornaments. Each square foot of booth space should provide the same amount of income to the project.

14 If you're serving food on the premises, keep it away from the area where the sales booths are located. Provide tables and chairs for the diners and keep your tables cleared of dirty dishes, napkins, etc. Long banquet size tables are best because at the more intimate, smaller tables, customers are more apt to sit and visit. The long tables are more impersonal and business-like. Have decorations on each table, carrying through the theme of the bazaar.

15 Everything but the perishable foods should be delivered to the sale place the day before the bazaar so it can be checked in, priced and displayed properly. Be sure you have enough workers on hand to keep this flowing easily. Have a specific "checking-in" time – for instance, from six until 10 the previous evening.

16 You should check to make sure proper lighting is available. Also, see that you don't put your fudge candies under the brightest lamp in the church basement – it melts. (I guess I have a thing about melted chocolate.) Make sure that the display tables won't tip over and that there aren't any electrical cords where customers (or workers) can trip over them.

17 Each booth should have proper change if there is no central payment place. Sometimes it's good to make arrangements with the local bank to have packets of $10 in change made up for each booth. Have one of your workers pick up these packets the morning of the sale. All workers should report for duty at least 30 minutes before the opening gun.

18 Make sure there is a reserved parking space close to the door for the car of your 'runner'. The runner is the one who runs to the grocery store to get more coffee cream, or to the bank for more change, or to the florist for more green tape for the wreath-making exhibition, etc. The car is also ready for any health emergency which might occur which is not serious enough for an ambulance. God-willing, you'll never have use for it, but again, be prepared. Remember that wonderful youth group, the Boy Scouts – and always Be Prepared!

A postscript for your runner – be sure there are two sets of keys to his/her car, just in case.

19 Have a couple of members or workers who are just 'floaters' who wander through the area, helping where help is needed – for instance, when too many customers are at one booth for the regular 'salesman' to handle.

20 Food leftovers can be sold at special prices to your workers or given to another worthy cause. Try to have a clean-up crew which is fresh and ready to take on the work of clearing away the debris, putting away tables, etc., so that those who have been manning the booths all day don't have to pull double duty. It doesn't always work that way, of course, but try. Sometimes your young members are better at manual labor than they are at one-on-one sales endeavors and will welcome this chore. It's another opportunity to give them a choice of what their share of the responsibility will be. I think we call that democracy.

21 Our second entry in the "hard work" field is STYLE SHOWS. There is little (except perhaps a new baby) which stirs the heart of a lady more than to see a display of beautiful new clothes – or even old, old clothes – most especially, wedding gowns.

So it stands to reason a style or fashion show is a great way to raise funds for your organization. It also stands to reason that you're going to have to have a commentator, models, clothing, a location, tickets, chairs, music, probably food, door prizes, programs, and decorations. This means a lot of work, but it's worth it.

22 The clothing can be provided by a local department store (they usually have a requirement that a minimum number of tickets be sold – several hundred) or made by talented home-seamstresses in the organization or community. (Your home economics class at high school usually has likely candidates for seamstress-models.) A style show featuring bridal gowns of any era is usually a sellout.

23 It is rather traditional that your members or their family members serve as models. You can include men's and boy's clothing, and the children are super models, precociousness and all. This also makes selling tickets easier because every grandmother (and lots of grandfathers, too) want to watch their tots come down the ramp. When the clothing is provided by a local store, fittings will be made by appointment. Your members will usually work with one or two of the store's employees who deal with fashion shows all the time and know all the in's and out's of the game. An incentive to the models is that the store will usually offer a good discount to any model who wishes to purchase the dress or outfit he/she models at the show! The store will also coordinate accessories for each outfit, and help make the overall effect of the parade of dresses, gowns and sportswear even more appealing to those who purchase tickets.

24 There may also be the possibility that the store will pay your organization a percentage of any sales made to viewers of the show, as a direct result of their attending your style show. Thus, you've made money from selling the viewer a ticket, and you may also make even more from the viewer purchasing a dress from the store! Is that double jeopardy? It's great for your treasury; that's for sure.

25 During the Bicentennial there were lots of historical gowns found hidden in attics and closets, and we were able to enjoy their various modes of simplicity or ornamentation. Those lovely gowns are still around. It's a super (although not new, admittedly) idea to show models in today's swim suits followed by the pantalooned bathing dress of the nineties and the tank suits of the twenties. Superimposing a lovely antique morning dress between models in today's office wear, or a ballgown of the last century among today's long gowns, is an intriguing way to study the history of fashions. It's also one of the most exciting ways I can think of to raise funds for your organization.

26 This is definitely a project where young models are not only desired, but absolutely necessary. Only today's tiny teens have the tiny waists and busts to fit those beautiful antique dresses. I had a waistline once, but that's another story and has little to do with fund raising, unless you count all the boxes of Rainbow candy I bought and ate – to help the cause, of course!

27 Advance ticket sales are a must for this project, especially if you're using commercial clothing and have a minimum seating to fill. You'll want to have a few nice door prizes for your guests. Use the ticket/stub secret we told you about in the previous chapter. In the program book, which will be passed out at the door to all the guests, be sure to list the names of the persons or businesses who donate the prizes.

28 The above paragraph assumes you have the following: (1) A committee to line up and pick up your prizes. Be sure to include your floral arrangements as part of your prizes, as they are already paid for or donated.
(2) A committee to attend at the door, i.e. take tickets, pass out program books and help people to their seats. There should be no reserved seats unless for the media, and older persons may need help.
(3) A committee which made up the tickets a long time ago and got them all sold.
(4) A committee which got the names of all the models, the descriptions of the clothing, names of all the gift donors and names of all the persons who played an integral part in the success of the day. Don't forget the commentator. All this information should be typed nicely into program booklet form and copies made (on a friendly office Xerox, remember?).
(5) A group of members at the very beginning of the whole thing who lined up the building, arranged for some type of music to accompany the show, made sure the chairs were set up, the ramp was up, the lighting was done and a few other million things which have to be done ahead of time – one of which is, as always, publicity.

29 The store which provides the clothing may or may not provide, or suggest, a commentator. The commentator is the person who reads the descriptions of all the outfits, introduces the models, and gives pertinent information, including cost, about the clothing. Sometimes a well-known local television or radio personality will donate his or her time to perform this function for your group, if you ask. Or it is quite likely you have a very suitable person for this job right there within your group, and by group, again, we include your members' families. There are many hidden talents and resources out there, right under your nose. Get to know your members and their families and you will find many, many treasures – and sometimes, often, a great commentator for your style show.

30 If possible you should have live music – organ, piano, or string trio. Again, try to get the music donated – this IS for a worthy cause. You probably can find some musical treasure within your own group, too, or you might find that recorded music works well. The worst possible thing is that you will have to hire an organist. But (don't tell anyone I said this) try to find a semi-professional so you won't have to pay too much. You're supposed to be raising money, not spending it.

31 This is another occasion when you should make a careful floor plan. Provide room for a runway or ramp, the commentator at one side of the stage with a lectern properly lit, a good sound system, musician(s), dressing rooms for the models, sufficient space for all the clothing to be carefully stored, how the chairs will be set up, where the tickets will be sold, where the door prizes will be displayed, and a few million other things you'll think of to add to your floor plan. Make sure, as with every function, that you know where the telephone is in case you need to make an emergency call, where the fire extinguishers are and where the exits are. Get to know the custodian of the building – you'll need to depend on him a lot. Safety first.

If you are required to promise the store a minimum of so many tickets sold, you need to have a space large enough to seat that many people. You can probably oversell your seats. There are always a few who don't show up. With advance ticket sales, you've already received their donation to your cause.

32 The store's representative will have last minute details for you and your models. Be sure they are all there at least a half hour before show time, and that the sound system is checked out in plenty of time. Check the ventilation, heating and air conditioning.

33 If you're serving food, have a distinct and separate committee take charge of that function. They need to know what accessories, such as tables, linens, and dishes, the facility can provide, and which they must arrange for. They proceed as for any other food service project, which is covered in other chapters.

34 The next long-range project you might take on is a STAGE PRODUCTION of some kind. Are you sure you want to do this? You need to decide *what* you want to do – a stage or musical show or a dance exhibition. For all of these, you must provide talent – either that of your members or of an amateur or professional group who will perform for you, at a fee or for a percentage.

35 If you choose to go the member-talent way, all I can say is good luck. You're braver than I, and I've braved a lot – and faked my way through a lot of fundraising. You need to have a director, a stage crew, a costume master or mistress, lighting crews, ushers, committees for publicity, tickets, and programs, a location with proper staging and seating, etc., and you have to have rehearsals and rehearsals and rehearsals. And patience and more patience. But, lots of people love this sort of thing and this makes it easy, or at least easier. If you love this sort of thing, you already know what you're in for, so you have my blessing. Break a leg!

36 If you don't have the talent within your group, you can go to a local school or to a theatrical agent. (Look in the Yellow Pages and let your fingers do the walking – all the way to the bank to deposit the money in your club treasury.) The agent can provide you with whatever type of theatrical production you would like. You line up the location and dates, do all the publicity (although often the agency helps with this), sell the tickets, buy one for yourself, sit back and enjoy the show. Unless, of course, you're a ticket taker or usher, in which case you'll get to see most of it. Keep in mind when you are dealing with agencies, that you will be dealing with contracts and union regulations, and it can get very complicated. So call in your friendly-lawyer-father for help again, to make sure you are not biting off more than you can chew. Keep in mind such things as minimum ticket sales requirements and use of union help in the building. Also keep an eye on some of the extras the contract may call for, which may eat away at the profits you want to keep in your club coffers for your worthy cause.

37 Stay away from those groups (rock bands seem to be the worst about this) who demand that special, expensive foods and beverages be kept backstage for them. Be sure that completely unnecessary demands are not included in the contract which you sign with them. Professional entertainers behave and act in a professional way and don't demand exotic foods which rob food from the mouths of the deprived children you may be trying to help.

In other words, when looking for a professional group, shop around and get those who are truly professional in every way. You can expect quality performances from them, on stage and off.

38 Other entertainments for which your group might plan and sell tickets include puppet shows, special showings of movies, classic film showings, lectures, concerts, and a few thousand others I've never even heard of. These are long-range projects in that they will require time to arrange bookings, locations, publicity, ticket sales, etc. It's up to your group whether to include food service, either provided in the cost of the ticket or per item by sale the night of the performance. If you pick the right project(s), your group can reap the benefits of someone else's talents and hard work.

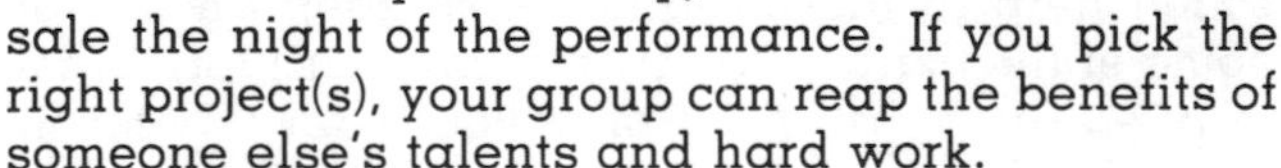

39 For any of these projects, try to line up patrons who will make donations toward paying for the booking and for the printing of programs, if required.

If you're presenting a really, really classy show you may decide you have to spend some money and have programs printed, especially if you wish to include the pictures of the performers. Photocopying is great, but it still doesn't reproduce pictures very well. Be sure to list the donors' names in the programs. This money should be collected at least three months prior to the performance.

40 As for any other performance or program, you may need to provide security, crowd control, and traffic control. Get acquainted with your local officials as we suggested earlier. They're great friends to have – in adversity and in times of raising funds for your favorite youth group.

41 Our next plan-ahead project is an EXHIBITION SPORTS event, such as a tennis match or pro-am golf tourney. You need about a year to do this, especially if it's your first time out. Maybe even a year and a half, to do it right. We did say 'long-range', remember?

This being America, you can always draw a crowd by staging a sports event. Promise some sports celebrities and you've got it made. Hence, the celebrity tennis match or pro-am golf tourney. Terrific fundraisers. Lots of planning and hard work.

42 Look to the promoters for help. Make sure, though, that you select promoters with proven track records and not fly-by-nights. There are a lot of the latter around, but they usually don't promote the real sports celebrities. They may promise the real sports celebrities, but if they can't deliver the bona fide signature of said celebrity on your contract, show them the door. There are too many of the legitimate promoters to even mess with the others.

43 Tickets for such events are not your $1 and $2 prices. Some TENNIS MATCH tickets sell for $35 or more for exhibition matches between top professionals. But in order to make this sort of money, you have to know what you're doing. So, the first time around, hire help. It's cheaper in the long run.

Remember that some athletic associations have firm rules about charity participation by their membership. Your match director is paid to know such requirements, so depend on him/her.

This is also a project which will require up-front cash for the site, talent, trophies, publicity, printing of tickets and programs, etc. Obviously, you need to start lining up donors for your charitable cause. Your director will help you decide what to charge for tickets (you can usually sell the programs separately); which souvenirs, if any, you will sell during the exhibition or tourney; and what you will do if it rains forty days and forty nights, and there isn't enough room on the ark for even three holes of golf.

44 If you have no idea how to get started on such a project, go to your local school or college athletic coach or to the golf course pro at the local greens. They may not know all the answers, but they will know who to send you to for advice and help.

45 Try to tie in other activities with the major event. A tennis exhibition could also include a mixed doubles match between your town's prominent citizens (perhaps the mayor and the coroner?) and two celebrities. This brings out even non-tennis buffs, just to see the city officials get creamed, and it sells more tickets.

46 If you're having a bowling tourney, see if you can't line up a really hot shot bowler for trick shots – if there is such a thing, truly. A bowling tourney could have an exhibition game of star bowlers on the first night, followed by local bowlers in the tourney rolling to top the score of the winning exhibition game(s). You might also include match games, benefit games, invitational tourneys, clinics and series of lessons during the week of your event.

47 If you can line up celebrities to attend or participate in your event, you've got a sure vote-getter and ticket-seller. Even if your local St. Louis Cardinals baseball player (that's my favorite team; you pick yours) can't bowl, he'll be an added attraction to your bowling tournament and help you sell tickets. Be sure to have your tourney in the winter when your baseball celebrity is between seasons and can give your group a helping hand. Check with your accountant. You can probably give your celebrity a receipt for X dollars of publicity which he can use for his own charity contribution on his 1040. And the kids will love meeting him and getting to know him.

48 You will need host families (or donating motel-hotel owners) to house the celebrities while they're in town. You will probably have all sorts of volunteers for this part of the action. Be sure you don't give all the choice celebs to the same members or families year after year. If you're housing a celebrity, remember you don't have to send him to the classiest home in your group's ownership. Most of them came from poor to moderate income families – as you and I. You're participating in a really sorry sort of discrimination if you pass up the third baseman on your little league team just because his folks have a two-bedroom home, and send your sports star to the wealthier, fancier home of the kid who usually sits on the bench. On the other hand, sometimes that kid who warms the bench needs a special kind of loving, too, and it's up to you, as their adult leader, to make this decision. It may be one of the toughest you'll ever make. Godspeed.

49 This sort of project will take, I repeat, lots of planning and lots of time and money up-front. It will also bring in tons of money. Depend on your tourney director, and use your own common sense when it comes to such things as meeting the participants at airports or train stations, escorting them to the game site, assigning them to their host families or hotels, and briefing them on your town and what's available to them in the way of historic sightseeing. Find out what their other interests are, and key their visit accordingly. You probably won't have to worry too much about their spending all their time in the local pub. They didn't get to be top athletes by bending their elbows, and they'll be more than ready to participate with you in YOUR town and your community. If at all possible, get your youth group together, and plan an activity when your celebrity can be with them.

50 For such events you need lots of workers, lots of record sheets and forms, prizes and trophies, a bonded treasurer (you will be handling lots of money), printed checks, a good accounting system, and first and foremost, someone who knows what he's doing. As I said before, hire a professional and do it right.

51 The last long-range project we'll talk much about is a CARNIVAL or FAIR. So, I'll be fair with you. You're going to be working pretty hard over the next several months if you're going the route where your group provides all the booths, all the activities, and everything the public will be buying tickets for to see and do. You will need lots of helpers, lots of booths, lots of ideas, and quite a bit of time for planning and for following through on your plans. Don't say we didn't warn you.

52 First of all, after you've selected your time and place, you need a theme. Countless thousands of carnivals have been planned around the circus theme. You might also use the county fair theme, or a holiday theme, or an ethnic theme. If you select a theme, it's usually easier to follow through with ideas for your booths and activities.

53 You'll need a minimum of ten booths. A minimum of twenty is better. See what I meant about needing workers? If you have an exceptionally small membership in your group, you'd better select some other way to raise your funds. Or include some other organizations, let them have some of the booths, and make it a cooperative affair.

54 The traditional fair combines entertainment and amusement with opportunities to purchase souvenirs or other items. The newer concept features exhibits and demonstrations of a cultural or ethnic nature and sometimes a puppet show, acrobatic act, or magician's act, or, preferably, all of these. The very concept of a fair or carnival means lots of activities, activities every way you look, and something for everyone – food, fun, games, and even a place to sit down and rest.

55 The booths can offer all of these but the place to sit down. A few well-placed benches can do that. Your booths can offer such activities as fortunetelling (complete with costumed gypsy), juggling, bowling, kissing and fishing. For the kissing booth take advantage of a friendly celebrity in your neighborhood and ask him or her to be the kissee. You'll boost your sales tremendously! Arrange for the fishing in a bowl or pond where kids can use a fishing pole with a large hook to try to pull a toy or prize out of a pile of prizes. If you have a large tank that will hold water, you can plant plastic fish. Let the kids pay to fish for them, and if they're successful, they then select their prize. You don't have to buy expensive prizes. Save some of the 'possibilities' from the rummage sale your group is having first – small toys and games, jewelry, or interesting books.

56 Other ideas for booths are handcrafted items and food items such as hot dogs and lemonade. (If at all possible, don't use powdered mix. The real thing isn't that difficult, and it's so much better.) Start with simple lemon syrup by combining 1 cup sugar, 1½ cups warm water and 1 tablespoon grated lemon peel. Add 1½ cups lemon juice or the juice from eight to 10 lemons. Cover and refrigerate. When you're ready to make lemonade, use ⅓ cup of the lemon syrup base to ⅔ cup cold water. Stir well, fill a 10-ounce paper cup with ice and add the lemonade. By the pitcher, add three cups lemon syrup to six cups water. Add cubes. Use this proportionately for your booth. It can be done ahead of time, and nothing beats the real thing – not even Coke.

57 One thing the kids can sell from their carnival booths might be BIRD FEEDERS. These can easily be made ahead of time by the members. For example, spray-paint a fine mesh colander to keep it from rusting (or use a plastic one), attach nylon line, fill it with sunflower seeds, and you have a feeder you can tie to the nearest tree limb.

58 Another feeder can be made by wiring pine cones together (use large to medium size cones) into a longish shape (approximately 10" x 3") with medium wire, and then coating it thickly with an inexpensive brand of peanut butter. Attach a hanger so it can be hung from a limb or hook.

59 Another idea would be to recycle a coconut into a cozy looking little bird feeder. Saw a square opening in the nut, about 3" x 3", remove the coconut, and then fill the shell with bird seeds, cereal or dried fruit. Attach a hanger at the top and hang the feeder from a tree.

60 Kids can easily make feeders from wire or string mesh bags, filling them with melted suet into which bird seed has been stirred. You have to let the suet firm up again before putting it into the mesh bags. Dried gourds also make excellent bird feeders or houses. Cut a small hole in the gourd, empty out the seeds and stringy pulp and attach a hanger.

61 You can even sell farms at your fair or carnival – ant farms. No need to invest in expensive kits from the toy stores. The kids can make their own and sell them to their friends. All it takes is two glass jars, one slightly smaller than the other, both with lids. Turn the smaller jar upside down and put it inside the larger one. Then fill the gap between the two jars with light sandy soil, but don't pack the soil in too tightly. All you need now is ants. Plan a picnic. Or, if you're tired of fried chicken and deviled eggs, put half a tablespoon of sugar in a half cup of water. Place it in the lawn where you have seen ants working. The sugar water will attract the ants and you can place ten or twenty of them in the sandy area of the jar you have just prepared. Screw the lid on securely, and once a week feed the ants about four drops of sugared water and a tiny crumb of bread. Don't feed them more than once a week, and don't punch holes (doors) in the lid. They will soon be building their tunnels in the sandy soil, and you'll have a ringside seat just outside the jars. Sell the instructions on how to care for the ants along with the 'ant farm' itself. These should sell for about $1 each, and all you have invested is a mayonnaise jar, an olive jar (both of which you would otherwise have thrown away), a tablespoon of sugar and a little time. Make these up two or three weeks ahead of time so the ants will have their farms started and clearly visible through the glass. Handle them with care and make a bundle selling ant real estate. Your booth sign can read "Real Estate – Cheap".

62 Another good seller for your fair or carnival is plants or herbs which the kids have raised themselves. The seeds can be started in egg cartons, and then the sections of the carton cut apart, to sell the seedlings. Planters can be made (and decorated with paints, left-over laces and rickrack) from plastic margarine and whipped cream cartons or from those plastic egg cartons in which we ladies buy our pantyhose. Drill holes on four sides, using a hot ice pick (adults only, please!), and attach ribbon or yarn for hangers. Decorate according to whim or theme.

63 Plants can be started in those small peat pots which come cheaper by the dozen, placed in muffin tins so they will not tip, and then sold separately in decorated planters. For planters, you can donate cups and saucers which no longer match anything in the kitchen, or some of the less interesting things you've ended up with after attending auctions or flea markets.

64 Other ideas for planters include cutting down plastic bleach or softener bottles, adding a scalloped or zigzag edge, and for a hanging basket, ribbon, wire or yarn for the hanger. Bend colored clothes hangers (two for each planter) into the reverse shape of a hydrogen balloon (you know – like "Around the World in Eighty Days") until it fits another plastic pot in which flowers are planted. The hooks are wrapped together to make one hanging hook for the planter. Use pliers to bend the hangers.

65 Another unique hanging basket for plants is made by using a pair of embroidery hoops wrapped with brightly colored raffia or yarn and secured top and bottom into an open ball shape. Inside this round frame you set a small planter, with a hanging vine such as vining begonia, and hang by more raffia.

66 A starter kit for plants can be made by using the bottom sectioned part of an egg carton (the pulpy paper kind). Fill the egg sections with sterile soil, set that section inside the top flat section (for added support), place a seed packet or two on top, and wrap with see-through plastic wrap and a bright ribbon.

67 All of the flowery items are displayed most favorably and appropriately if you can come up with a flower cart display booth, similar to those in the Parisian markets. Look up an old Gene Kelly movie if you've forgotten what they look like.

68 A game for your carnival can be a clothespin drop, in which the kids buy tickets to drop so many clothespins into a milk bottle or carton. Winners get a prize. Once again, the prizes need not be expensive ones.

69 For your carnival it's a good idea to sell the long strings of tickets which you can buy from theatres or advertising firms, using a base of 5 or 10 cents each. The tickets are usable at any booth on the grounds. It might take only 1 ten-cent ticket for a game of clothespin drop, and ten tickets for a hot dog. It's easier for the smaller children to hold on to than money, and they have great fun spending their tickets.

70 Another carnival booth might have yarn art which the kids have made by dragging a paint-dipped piece of yarn across plain or colored paper. Thumbkin paintings are sold by letting the customer dip his thumb on the colored ink stamp pad, and then placing the impression on a piece of plain paper. Your member, with a modicum of art, adds features such as arms, legs, hats, tails, or whatever, and makes creatures called Thumbkins.

71 Other artwork might include prints made with potatoes or sponges into which a pattern has been cut. The pattern is then inked with a stamp pad, placed on the paper, and the art is ready. This is a great thing to remember at Christmas time, when you're all out of wrapping paper and you need yards more. Make your own – or better yet, let the kids do it – using the potato or sponge impressions.

72 A bowling game can be made by using empty milk cartons and a tennis ball. Be sure to have a good backstop to catch the action.

73 A wandering photographer with an instant camera and a lot of film can sell action shots of the kids. For added zest, dress him (or her) in black like a nineteenth century photographer. Give him an assist with a contraption like the old-time magnesium 'flash cube' which was held over the head and set off with a bright flash for lighting. It can be made easily by attaching a small rubber hose between a small supply of flour hidden under the assistant's clothing and a mason's mortar board with a squeeze bulb (also hidden) which sets off the explosion of flour-magnesium every once in a while. The mortar board is the part held high to give the lighting effect.

74 A really spectacular idea for a booth is called Instant Ancestors. All you need are several pieces of plywood or fiber board into which is cut, at the top, a half circle (to place your chin on) and on which are painted pictures of men and women in old-fashioned dress. Plan on one board with two people on each side, and two boards with only one person on each side. Choose a George and Martha Washington couple, perhaps, and an Indian squaw and brave on the reverse. The singles can be a pioneer man with his long rifle and buckskin clothing and a World War II sailor on the reverse. The feminine board might be the counterparts – a pioneer woman and a jitterbugging girl of the forties, complete with bobby socks and saddle shoes. Have real hats to add to the picture: a tricorn and white ruffled mobcap for George and Martha, an Indian warbonnet and single feather and headband for the Indians, a coonskin cap and sunbonnet for the pioneers, a large red hair ribbon for the bobby soxer, and a white sailor hat for the seaman (and don't forget to paint him bowlegged – all sailors are bowlegged, aren't they? – or is that only Popeye?).

Now all you need is a photographer with an instant camera and a supply of film, and a bunch of customers who want their pictures taken behind your cleverly painted ancestor boards. Charge according to your expenses – cost of film plus time and a little for the paint and plywood or fiber board scenery. Be sure you have a good sized sign advertising your INSTANT ANCESTORS!

75 If you have a kissing booth, decorate it accordingly with hearts and lip prints all over the place. If you have a celebrity to pucker up for you, you've got it made. You might have a comic option – if you can find a grandparent willing to show up without their teeth – by offering Granny's (or Gramps') gummies to anyone unable to stand the power of a real pucker. Even a sign advertising such (with a drawing of a toothless hag) will add laughter and attention to your booth. You could offer your kisses at two different prices. For the smaller price, they get a foil-covered Hershey's chocolate kiss. But be sure you're making a profit on each piece of candy, too. Remember that you're raising funds for a good cause, and anything goes – well, almost anything. You just don't have to tell that the $5 kisses are real and the $1 ones are chocolate. Your sign could read "Strawberry Kisses, $5" (and try to have your pretty girl wear strawberry flavored lipstick) and "Chocolate Kisses, $1". Then, you've been honest about the whole thing. Honest.

76 Something else your young members might like to make to sell at their fair would be dolls made from wooden spoons. The faces are painted on, caps or bandana head coverings tied on, with a long skirt to cover the handle in a sort of pioneer design. If well-made, these bring anywhere from $4 on up, and can be made and priced according to the size and price of the original spoon.

77 If you have a resident artist in your group (remember what we keep preaching about using the resources you have), set up a booth where customers can have caricatures or sketches of themselves made. An easel with artist at work draws a lot of attention, and almost everyone wants to see what they look like in an artist's eye. If the artist is really good and usually charges a large fee for her work, work out a percentage basis. And, of course, if he or she is willing to donate the work to your cause, all the better.

78 Another great idea for a booth for the kids to operate is a clay booth. There they can not only sell items they have created from their homemade clay, but they can sell jars of colored clay, or, for a smaller amount, the recipe for making the clay at home. The clay recipe is as follows: Combine 1 cup salt, a half cup flour and 1 cup of water in a saucepan. Heat over low heat until thick and rubbery. Cool on a cookie sheet. If the dough seems sticky, add a little more flour. Use it right away or store it in an airtight container. Once you have made your "clay-ation" (clay-creation), it can be air dried until it's hard. Kids can make animals, jewelry, tree ornaments, candlesticks, bowls, vases, ashtrays, and all sorts of things from this inexpensive clay. It can be painted with poster paint.

79 Another good selling item is clothespin dolls. They can be made as Christmas tree ornaments or residents of doll houses. Tiny bits of fabric can turn a small round-headed pin into quite a lovely doll, with just a bit of imagination. Turn the little girls (and enlist grandmother's aid, if possible) loose with this project and watch them create. Even the boys may enjoy making toy soldiers, sailors, or pioneers from these sturdy, inexpensive items.

80 Remember that one way to get a lot of small items made for your various booths is to create an assembly line for each project. This way, each child/member does one part of the work and then passes it on to the next to add another touch, and so on. This is at your meetings, of course, before the sales event.

81 Other easy things to make for sale at your booths are plain anklets dressed up with bows in the school colors or with lace or tiny appliqués. Why not an alligator to match the ones on your shirt? Purses can be made easily by using ready-made quilted place mats and a little imagination. Stuff that one-only glove and stitch it closed, add ribbon and lace, and voilà, you have a pretty little pin cushion. What else can you do when you lose the other glove?

82 Got a bunch of tee shirts you've outgrown, and they have your favorite slogan on the front? Stitch the openings shut, stuff with 'stuffing' or worn out nylon stockings, and make a pillow which you can keep for your own room or the kids', or sell it at your fair booth. Some people even add embroidered stuffed heads and limbs and make shirt people out of shirts. Don't even try to make the heads and limbs the appropriate size, though; they're much more interesting when they're really weird!

83 More pillows can be made by purchasing inexpensive plain colored ones and appliquéing them with those handmade crocheted lace doilies everyone has lying around in drawers but never uses. These bring high boutique prices. Price at least double the price of your purchased plain pillow. Use other bits and pieces of left-over lace and trim on other plain pillows. Dress them up and make a bundle for your organization.

84 If you want to make skirts and have a good supply of material lying around, cut two rectangles of fabric forty-five to sixty inches wide, and in various lengths (according to the heights of your possible customers). Add three inches for casing and hem. Sew the sides together, make a casing at the top (which will be 45" or 60" x 2" wide, less your seam width) through which you run elastic. Hem, that's it. If you prefer a prairie skirt, cut the rectangle fairly long and attach a four inch flounce at the bottom. The flounce should be twice the hem circumference. These are best in denims, plaids and stripes to carry out the prairie theme. Easy.

85 These are just a few of the ideas we've come up with for your carnival or fair. Mostly they're old ideas, just spruced up a bit. As usual, our advice is – use your imagination. If someone has a nice, gentle pony, by all means, have a pony ride. Just be sure you don't put it next to the shooting gallery, and also be sure you aren't breaking any zoning ordinances by having an animal at that particular location. Another thing about ponies is that you need a shovel once in a while to keep your act from being X-rated. And, finally – about ponies – they can be stubborn. If your star Trigger balks, give up and just let him be something to pet (change your sign and lower your price), and that's more than most of your young customers have at home. They'll love him, anyway.

86 Another thing you might rent "your" space for is a FARMER'S MARKET, held during the summer months on successive weeks, or on a one-time-only basis at the height of truck-garden harvest time.

5 Your Junk or Mine?

Flea Markets; Rummage Sales; Garage Sales; Merchandising Ideas; Pricing; Leftovers

Your Junk or Mine?

Tradition says that King Henry II, way back in 1312, banned peddlers from the streets of London, because he was sure they were the cause of the infestation of fleas. The citizens of London took up the cry, referring to the campsites just outside the town as "flea markets." The peddlers either had no defense or just didn't care about the nasty nomenclature. Either way, they prospered, just as did the Parisian ragpickers across the English Channel, who gathered in that city's northern district and set up their stalls to sell their wares. Today, approximately 3,000 stalls are spread over four square miles in Paris, and "Le Marche Aux Puces" is a major tourist attraction.

Not until the late 1950's did flea markets migrate to America. A Connecticut Yankee dealer staged what he called the "Original One-Day Rural Flea Market" for a charity group's fundraising effort. That first flea market had only 80 dealers, but the idea flourished. Today, many drive-in theaters rent out their flat space during the day for a modest fee to persons or groups who set up their tables, fold down car tailgates, display their wares, and make a small profit, often from items gleaned from closets, attics and garages.

87 Your group may choose to make money by taking family rummage to a flea market and setting up your own table(s). Or, you may have a garage sale in someone's garage to sell all of the accumulated junk and treasures which have been donated to your cause.

88 As with all your other ventures into raking in the funds for your group, you need to advertise. Many newspapers even provide brightly colored posters for you to put up in the community, if you purchase an ad in their classified columns. One thing about signs in the neighborhood – in case we haven't already mentioned it – if you put them up, be sure you take them down. It's a courtesy you owe to your community, and who wants customers showing up on Monday for a sale that ended on Saturday evening?

89 Clothing, toys, and kitchen items are all things families accumulate and ultimately need to dispose of. It will take your group about two months to line up merchandise and do the proper promotion for a successful rummage or garage sale. Don't try to sell winter coats in May or bathing suits in September. Those who do their shopping at garage sales don't buy that far in advance, and you're just wasting valuable space by selling such out-of-season items. You may have a great supply of perfectly beautiful long dance dresses, but they won't sell in June. Proms are over, and school dances for next fall are a long way off. If you can have an inside sale in March, then you can move that merchandise, but not in June.

90 You will need to have a clean, open space to hold your sale, with tables set up for display. A good display idea is to place your items on bench type heights where they are easy to see. Unless you have acres of room, don't put your merchandise on the ground. It will get stepped on or overlooked; under your tables is even worse. Cover your tables with sheets and use the underneath for storing boxes, sacks and cord which will be used to pack your customers' purchases. It makes for a much neater display, too.

91 Each piece should be clearly marked. You might also have a sign that reads "All Remaining Articles Drastically Reduced During Last Two Hours Of Sale". Another winning sign reads, "We Don't Mind If You Laugh At Our Junk!"

92 You will need a good committee to check in all the items, to price them, and to place them on your display tables. If at all possible, ask your members to have their items marked BEFORE they bring them to the sale. This saves hours of work which could be put to better use and helps distribute the chore. Make certain they all have a master list of suggested prices for your items. If you want to stay away from customers who want even more of a bargain than you're offering (so they change the prices on your items), staple the prices onto the item. Be sure, though, that your labels or staples do not do damage to your merchandise. If people complain about having to get the labels or gummy stuff off, advise them to use vegetable oil which does a great job of softening the label so it can be easily removed.

93 Be sure your merchandise is clean. A box of glasses, however pretty or useful, will not bring as much (or perhaps even sell) if it is displayed in a dusty, saggy-bottomed box, with the glasses themselves covered with months of basement dirt and soot. Clothing should be washed and, if necessary, ironed. You might take an iron with you, if your sale's inside, to smooth out some of the worst wrinkles in the better items. It may double the sale price of your item. Keep an eye on your iron, so it doesn't get sold!

94 The sale price – ah, here's the rub. Don't be a pig about prices. Remember that old saying about a bird in the hand, because this is a time when it certainly applies. You may feel that that old television set is worth fifty dollars. But since you're not about to guarantee anything at a sale like this (unless it was yours and you absolutely know it worked the last time it was plugged in), if you get offered twenty-five dollars, and the sale is near the halfway mark, don't blink your eye. Grab the offered dough, point to the set and say, "It's yours!" Otherwise, it may still be there at the end of the day, even though you've marked it down to fifteen dollars.

95 If a customer makes an offer on something, don't be too quick to say that it's not enough. If it means – as it often will – the difference between a sale and the item being left at the altar, grab the offer. Your overhead at this sale isn't going to be too great, remember, so you can afford to be charitable, too. And every nickel that goes into the cashbox brings you that much closer to your goal.

96 Speaking of your cashbox, you should probably plan to have twenty-five to fifty dollars in quarters and ones, with a few dollars in nickels and dimes. It should be kept by a responsible member, and it should be kept closed and out of sight. Don't place temptation in anyone's face.

97 If you have a lot of nice clothing, provide a curtained corner with a mirror for fitting. You can use folding screens for this purpose, or set up a couple of stepladders which you drape with blankets or sheets.

98 Stepladders are also excellent ways to display your smaller items. All you need is two stepladders of the same size. Set them up so the step sides face each other, get boards approximately the width of the steps, place them from ladder to ladder, and you have instant shelves.

99 We mentioned placing your packing supplies under the display tables, and perhaps you wondered about the cord. If you have a large piece of furniture, say a chair or smallish dresser, having a cord to tie down a car trunk lid may make the difference between selling that piece or having it as a left-over. Don't forget the cord.

100 If you can make a sale of a large item dependent upon getting it moved, use your transportation committee. The transportation committee is obviously made up of the members of your group who have a pick-up truck, van or large station wagon. You're using your resources again. You may not need to put them to work at all, but it's nice to know they're there, just in case. The pick-ups are handy for hauling the stepladders, tables and other display stuff, too.

101 If you're holding your sale outside, plan on a rain date, just in case. Your posters should give clear, concise directions for reaching the sale site, and it's a good idea to say "Absolutely no early sales" unless you're prepared to have sales personnel on hand to deal with people who arrive hours too early. They're really a pain in the neck if you're busy trying to price items and get them displayed properly, so we strongly suggest "no early sales".

102 If you have some really classy items for your sale, include them by name in your ad in the newspaper. If you have one antique, the ad should read 'antiques'. Antique buyers also buy junk, remember, so be sure to lure them to your sale. If they're antiquers, they're also junkers at heart, so you really aren't doing any false advertising. If someone absolutely says, "But there's only ONE antique in the whole sale, and your ad said plural!", show them your driver's license which has your true age on it. This will demonstrate YOUR antique status. That is quite a sacrifice toward your cause, but you're doing this for charity, remember. You could be canonized for it.

103 Make sure your work crew shows up in plenty of time to help – which, freely translated, means at least an hour before the sale starts. This also gives them time to do their own shopping to get the choice items for themselves before the crowd arrives. Be sure they pay for what they buy. This rummage sale is for the group, not an individual enterprise, so the time for swapping items is long past.

104 If you have some really nice little left-overs which could be used at your group's carnival for prizes (and if one of your members is willing to store them until carnival time), by all means, save them. It will save your having to line up prizes at carnival time. Otherwise, it's often easy to call the local Salvation Army or Goodwill and have their truck arrive at closing time to cart off what didn't sell. And you're aiding another good cause. That way, there is no repacking, no carrying home, no storing of those large items until your next sale.

6 Booths Even Lincoln Would Love

Rent-a-space Ideas; Antiques; Art, Crafts, Raffles, Collector Shows; Selling Tickets, Legal Ramifications

Booths Even Lincoln Would Love

105 Booths play an important part in fundraising. In Europe they're called kiosks. Such little stands can be set up in almost any setting to sell almost anything. They can be decorated to carry out a theme or just be plastered with signs advertising the wares and prices. They can be put-up and take-down structures or so solid that an earthquake couldn't faze them. They can be faked by imaginative fundraisers who use whatever is at hand to come up with a little space that is surrounded by counters and usually covered to keep out the weather. Or they can be elaborate, multi-faceted shacks with all the amenities of home-sweet-home (like electrical outlets, built-in sinks, refrigerators, stoves and deep fryers). They can be tables under an awning or just umbrella tables. Resources. Use your resources. You can create quite a nifty little booth for your sales effort with what you have. Don't spend a lot of money unless you have an angel who's footing the bills or you've inherited great-grandmother's favorite little booth – both of which are highly unlikely.

106 At the back of this book we have shown dimensions and sketches of a booth which is easy to build, put up, take down and store, and doesn't cost an arm and a leg. But, you don't have to have a fancy booth to sell your merchandise. It helps, but it isn't one of the necessities of life.

107 One of the best things about booths is that you don't have to own or create a single booth to make a mint of money. Let other vendors set up their booths in space you have rented to them. You can hold your own flea market, art show, antique show, collector's show, craft show or any other kind of show where people can exhibit or sell their wares. They do almost all the work while you and your group take a goodly sum to the bank.

108 Of course, for such a project, first you have to have the space. Space comes free (usually) from churches, schools, fraternal organizations, or sometimes even your town, to hold a charitable fundraising event. If your group is affiliated with any of the above groups, you're already in the front door. If not, usually all it takes is a request. You may have to pay for such items as janitor service, electricity, etc., but these are affordable expenses compared to the profit you can make from holding your own 'show' or sale, i.e. selling spaces for others to show and/or sell.

109 If you're holding your event inside, the weather won't make too much difference. You obviously won't schedule it for blizzard or monsoon seasons, anyhow. But if you're going for the great out-of-doors, there's always rain which dampens more than the spirits of those trying to sell their wares or exhibit their collections. If your event is scheduled for outside, have a rain date. This is vital, because you've already sold your spaces, collected your rental fees, and signed contracts with your vendors long before the actual date of the event. If you have rented them a space, you have to be able to deliver. Hence, the rain date.

110 Your spaces should be at least ten to twelve feet wide, and the depth depends on the space you have available to sell. This is very obviously a venture in which you absolutely, no doubt about it, positively have to have a floor plan. You need to carefully measure your space before you sell the spots, so you can do the proper dividing and multiplying (if they need more than one space). You need a method of marking off each location – yellow chalk to mark concrete, masking tape markers on sides of buildings, large rocks at the corners of each space, or you may think of better ways.

111 The contract you and each vendor signs (don't forget to have it checked over by that lawyer we mentioned earlier) should indicate the size of their space, the number and exact location (number your spaces on your floor chart so you can easily locate any spot you want to), the amount of payment, and any other particulars (including the rain date). If you are providing the tables and (at least) two chairs, the contract should so state. If the vendor must supply his own display items, the contract must say so. The hours of the sale should be on the contract, as well as any local ordinances which might apply and what absolutely cannot be sold from the booths. (Perhaps your village, like ours, is a dry township – no homemade beer or wine, please.) Your lawyer helper may advise you of other items to include in your contract. The contracts should be sent out several (perhaps even many) months prior to the show or sale date with a deadline for payment. If the vendor doesn't show up at the last minute, you already have received the payment for his space so it isn't a total loss just because it's too late to rent to another. In fact, no-shows are the reason you insist on advance payment. You can't just run out in the street and flag down someone to take that space, and selling space is what you're doing.

112 Some courtesies you may want to extend to your vendors are little slips of paper or coupons entitling them to two cups of free coffee, or a free donut and coffee, if you intend to set up your own little kiosk to sell donuts and coffee to those who come to buy and sell that day.

113 Our little (tiny) Sangamo Chapter of Eastern Star at Rochester began such an event by hosting an antique show and sale by renting the cafeteria of the local school and then renting spaces to antique dealers. Overnight security was provided so no break-ins or pilfering could occur, the organization served sandwiches and homemade cakes and pies for lunch, and a great time was had by all. In fact, there was celebration on the way to the bank the next day.

114 Called the Harvest Fair, the Star group also sponsors a pumpkin pie baking contest and, in the local primary school, an art contest, with winners given ribbons and small prizes. The contests help swell the crowds, and the organization banks several hundred dollars – often more – and a great time is had by all. If your group has such space available for their use, come up with an idea of how to use it for your fundraising purposes.

115 If you don't want to sell pies and cakes, make it ice cream cups (the dairy provides packing, spoons, etc. – almost all but the manpower to sell it) or soft drinks kept cold in an iced livestock watering tank (borrow it from your neighborhood dealer and be sure to put up a large sign letting everyone know of his generosity – it's good business for both of you).

116 Or, you can easily sell hot dogs if you have a charcoal grill or two, or a couple of large electric roasters – one for the hot dogs and one for the buns. Keep it simple or make it fancy. That part is up to you.

117 Another thing you can rent your space for is an art show. You can do this one of two ways – use only the work of professional artists and deal with a gallery or agent, or, open it to any talented artists. You know your community and you know your resources. Go from there.

118 The art offered for sale and display should be varied, from oil paintings and water colors to graphics, sculpture, and perhaps even a broader variety than that. Graphics such as woodcuts, lithographs, etchings, screen prints, and engravings are usually less expensive and therefore sell well. You may want to include photos, too, if you have such artwork available in your community or can lure it there. Some of the pictures should be framed, some not.

119 It will take approximately two to three months to get such a show on the road. It is best to have it inside, such as in a large hall or gymnasium. Outside is okay if the weather cooperates. Again, you will need a rain date if you're selling space outside. You should decide whether to have a one-day show or a weekend one. Weekend runs are usually better.

120 If you have questions about putting on such a show, contact your local art association, art supply shops, or any private collector with whom you may have contact. It is always nice to have art supplies (displayed artistically, of course), art books, or perhaps a portrait sketcher on hand, and they help increase total sales income.

121 You will probably want to hold some sort of reception for your artists in connection with your art show. A tea or cocktail party would be appropriate.

122 Expenses for your art show can run into the thousands of dollars if you let it, depending on the scope of the show and the cooperation of local donors in providing free services and supplies. You should have programs which list all the pieces on exhibit and the names and credentials of the artists. If you have an angel to pay for your program booklets, keep his or her wings polished, for such a booklet is an asset to any art show and can itself become a collector's item. If you are lucky enough to have a really super booklet for your program, it can include photos of the artists and some of their work. Again, you can't do this type of copying on your office Xerox machine, as great as they are.

123 You should have insurance to cover the art work, or your contract should clearly state that the artist is responsible for damages sustained to his art work. See your attorney pal again – it's vital. The artists decide on the prices for their paintings. Your contract should provide for a percentage of the selling price, usually ten to twenty percent.

124 There are two ways of dealing directly with artists. One way is to keep one-third of the sales price and the other is to charge the artists according to the size of the space they utilize. If you're keeping one-third of the sales price, you will probably find that the most popular items are priced in the $15 to $25 range for graphics and up to $200 for oil paintings. Obviously some of the works will be more expensive, but probably some of them will sell, if you and your publicity committee have done your job properly.

125 You will need several committees to carry on your art show including a vigilante (hanging) group. The proper placement of the art work is vital to the aesthetics of the show and, while most of the artists who bring their work will have their own very rigid ideas, you should have the final word concerning whether two exhibits create confusion or an unpleasing overall look to the total show. You will definitely need a security detail if you're holding an overnight show, regardless of any insurance provisions. An ounce of prevention pays off.

126 A craft show, or exhibition of any particular or varied items, can be handled in the same way. The nearby Methodist Church at Edinburg has held a very successful quilt show for several years. Quilters are urged to exhibit their new or heirloom quilts, and the quilts are displayed on the wall, across the backs of the church pews and on special hangers. A lovely quilt is either donated by an individual, or paid for from the proceeds of the day and raffled off to a lucky, lucky, holy gambler. Tickets are sold which include a superb salad luncheon served in the church dining room during specific hours of the exhibit. Quilts are a craft of the past which seem to be having a rebirth, and isn't that great! Your group's members can go to bed with a smile on their faces at night (under their own downy quilts), if they're lucky enough to have access to quilters and quilts, and can deal with a little work in publicity, selling tickets, and making salads for that luncheon. Try it – you'll like it!

127 One thing about raffles – they may be illegal in your state. Often a charitable fundraiser is benignly neglected by the enforcement arm of the attorney general's office as are office baseball pools. But don't run the risk of any embarrassment to your organization if you know it is a rigidly enforced law in your neck of the woods. See what the precedent is before you dive into that particular pool.

128 If raffles are legal in your vicinity, they offer any number of opportunities for raising funds for your group. You offer virtually anything from sides of beef to television sets, CB radios, furs, trips to exotic places, and you name it. People are now even selling their homes that way, by combining with a charitable group and sharing the proceeds. Dealing with a raffle can be dangerous. You must be certain your tickets are non-reproduceable, that they have some means of identifying the proper winner when the final drawing is held, that all the taxes are paid by the winner (have a contract for him to sign), and that your organization has complied with any applicable laws or ordinances. You can raise thousands of dollars by raffles, and as a result they require more care, more security, more publicity, and sometimes more worry. It's your decision.

129 You could even hold a car show or a show limited to beer can collections or any kind of collection, if it's something people will come to see. You can raise your funds by selling tickets to the people who want to see your show, or you can charge the exhibitor for the space he's using. Decide which will work better in your area.

The space program doesn't necessarily deal with only folks like Neil Armstrong and Buzz Aldrin. It deals with you and your organization and how you can raise funds for your worthy cause. It's one of the more important resources you have at your disposal. Use it accordingly.

7 Target Days: Will You Hit the Bullseye?

Rent-a-kid or Slave Days; Celebrity Auction; Dunk Tanks; Marathons; House or Garden Tours

Target Days: Will You Hit the Bullseye?

By target, we mean a specific day for a specific thing. Such an event might be a Slave Day, Rent-A-Kid Day, Celebrity Auction, Marathon, or House or Garden Tour. These are all super ways to bring in the dollars for your club coffers. Have I mentioned the egg yet?

130 SLAVE DAY is a day set aside (usually a Saturday) when your neighbors all know (because of your excellent publicity committee) that they can call a central number and arrange for a member of your group to come and do a specific household chore such as wash windows, paint a fence, put up or take down the screens and/or storm windows, rake the lawn, clean the attic, basement or camper, or whatever else they haven't had time to do themselves. The hourly rate is the same for every job, or you can just do it on a donation basis, whichever you feel would work best in your community.

131 If you are working with a youth organization (aren't we all, at one time or another?), the "RENT-A-KID" name takes on a certain aura of excitement. Your advertising should be started well in advance of the day, so appointments can be made in plenty of time. You'll need to know how much work is in store and how many members you'll need to fill all the requests. An excellent way to provide the appropriate telephone number is to put many of them at the bottom of your poster, on little fringe-like strips cut vertically, so potential customers can tear off one little strip on which the number is legibly printed. You can cut anywhere from ten to thirty of these strips at the bottom of your poster, depending on its size.

132 Try not to assign a member to one hard job all day. If it is one of those particularly boring or tough jobs, you may lose the member to exhaustion as well as his or her membership in your group. Spread out the tasks. As an example, send out several crews to paint that mile of fence your neighbor wants whited. Don't ask the same people to do the same thing all day. Unless, of course, they prefer it that way. Remember to give them that choice we talked about before.

133 Make sure there is a specific time for your members to report to the job and to return to the central command post. (That's where the main telephone number is and where you, or a responsible member, know, at any given moment, where each and every member of your group can be found, in case of an emergency and for the members' own safety.) Customers should be made to understand that if their particular chore is scheduled to be done late in the afternoon, due to the multitude of job orders, it may not be possible to complete it that day, but that your member or members will return no later than the next Saturday to complete the job. Obviously, you wouldn't schedule anything late in the day which can't be left undone, like windows being taken out and not replaced, etc. Whoever is in charge of the scheduling of the jobs should have some idea of how much time is required and place it on the day's agenda accordingly.

134 Be sure your members don't wear their very best bib and tuckers when reporting to work. Just a couple of spots of paint can ruin a new outfit quickly and that won't endear your project to a certain mother. Neither should your volunteer workers show up looking like they robbed the local ragpicker. Their clothing should be clean, comfortable, practical and geared to the weather and the possible chores they may be performing.

135 This is a project for which you will probably need a transportation committee, particularly if the members are too young to drive themselves or have no access to a car. And it's important that your transportation committee remember thay they have to return the child to the command post or home after the day's work is done! Don't leave some kid out in the boondocks without transportation. It's bad for the morale. Some of them would be scared to death (and perhaps have reason to be), and it's poor planning and follow-through on the part of you and your organization. Finish what you start.

136 A CELEBRITY AUCTION is another example of a target day. Line up as many celebrities as you can – the mayor, city or state (or, if you're lucky, national) elected officials, sports stars, media personalities, or your next-door movie star. Ask them what service they would be willing to donate toward your cause. If they don't have an idea, dream up your own: Have the mayor serve a candlelight dinner for four in his home. Get the school principal to agree to drive your family and friends to a local restaurant for dinner. Perhaps you could use the big yellow school bus (you'll need permission for that), or he could wear a chauffeur's uniform and drive a rented limousine. The limousine can be donated by the livery service in town; the bus can be loaned by the bus company. The mayor provides the food, or perhaps the owner of the local grocery store will donate it. It will take several months – plan on at least two – to line up all the donors and participants in the Celebrity Auction.

137 Then, be sure you get lots of publicity. This is easy to do when celebrities are involved, because, let's face it, the television camera is much more familiar with their faces than it is with ours, and they just naturally start rolling when a star strolls into view. Set up your press meeting, have a few of your celebrities on hand to agree publicly to all the gimmicks, and you'll get the publicity. Sell tickets to your Celebrity Auction for a nominal fee if some of your celebrities are famous, important or popular enough to have fans wanting their autographs. If the celebrity is willing to sign little slips of paper during the auction, you'll have people buying tickets just to get to meet their favorite sports star, while others will be showing up to bid on the services offered by the celebrities.

138 Have the auction in a location which is inspiring. A school in Springfield has theirs at the Governor's Mansion and you can't beat that for atmosphere, unless you have access to the White House lawn.

139 Just in case, you should have a simple, perhaps lightly-written (as in humorous) contract drawn up by your ever-helpful attorney, with space for the celebrity to list what service he will perform and what commodities will be provided within the frame of time specified. This contract should, of course, be signed. It wouldn't be very good publicity if your club were to have to take legal action in case the celebrity failed to follow through on the service for which he was "auctioned off." But, on the other hand, the celebrity, if he has any stature at all, would not want the adverse publicity which would result from a no-show.

And while we're talking about the "fun" of fundraising, we also have to keep track of the community spirit which results from it, or the lack of spirit in case of a real failure on the part of someone to follow through on his or her obligation.

140 Another way to take advantage of the soft heart of a local (or available) celebrity might be at a fair or carnival dunk tank where the celebrity perches, in bathing attire, above a tank of water and is unceremoniously dunked when a ticket purchaser hits the target with a ball. Tanks can be rented in most parts of the country. Contact a public relations firm or even your own chamber of commerce or library to get in touch with someone who can rent you such a booth.

Just as there is larceny in the hearts of most of us, so there is this nasty little craving to see our social, economic or political superiors doing menial labor – or looking ridiculous – just by our spending a buck or two toward a good cause.

141 Another target day could be a MARATHON. It doesn't have to be the "They Shoot Horses, Don't They?" kind of dance marathon. You can hold a marathon of any event, even one as simple as rocking in a rocking chair. The craze for physical fitness provides a perfect background for bike-a-thons, or other 'thons' where participants jog, run, walk, swim, skate, or even yo-yo.

142 The money is raised prior to the event by the participants calling as many friends and relatives as they can and lining up pledges – often for as little as 5¢ an hour or mile, or whatever. The participants then collect the increments, multiplied by the completed units of accomplishment, after the marathon is over.

Confused? Well, let's say we're having a bike-a-thon. Five cents is the pledge donation, and one participant bicycles ten miles during the given time, earning fifty cents. If that cyclist has taken pledges from ten relatives, then each of the ten sends the cause fifty cents, and the total received from one participant's efforts is five dollars. Multiply such amounts by many, many participants, and many, many pledges, and you can raise a lot of money for your special cause. It's usually good to have some prizes for the participant who outdoes all the others in either pledges or miles or a combination of the two. Perhaps you would want prizes given in those categories according to age groups, and naturally you'll try to get the prizes donated by local merchants. A bicycle or a trophy would certainly be an appropriate prize for the overall highest fundraiser in your bike-a-thon.

143 Marathons are one of the ways you can use your imagination and utilize a lot of talent or non-talent in your community. Even I would volunteer to sit and rock (if you give me a stack of books and a cup of coffee once in a while) in a marathon. If you have sports-minded resources (people) make it a sports-a-thon. If lazy, unathletic resources (citizens) are all you have around you, don't despair. Rock like crazy. Old fogies can raise just as much money in a marathon as super jocks can. And probably brag more. It's called community spirit when you get everyone involved. Also fun. Can you imagine your high school gym filled with all sizes and shapes of rocking chairs (not to mention folks) all rocking away? Quick, call the television station. This is definitely something you need to see to believe. But it's one easy way to raise funds.

144 Another event which could come under the heading of a target day could be a HOUSE or GARDEN TOUR. For this you obviously need people with fabulous homes or gardens who are willing to open them to the public during a given period, just to help your group raise money. Because most of us have this terrible curiosity about how the other half lives, it's easy to sell tickets for such tours. This way, you pay a nominal fee and get to peek at how the Jones' keep up, without being forced to peek in their windows.

145 The typical house or garden tour should include at least four places of interest, perhaps historical, renovated or ultra-modern homes, or homes interesting for their architectural design. If you have a garden tour, the gardeners will know the best time of the year – spring, summer or fall – for the tour, depending on the floral contents of their lovely gardens.

146 The exact path for the tours should be (must be) roped off or carefully defined in other manners, to avoid trespass by too-enthralled visitors who would otherwise check out the closets, all the bathrooms, and underneath the rose bushes.

147 There should be two hostesses (or hosts) in each room if there are particularly expensive or valuable objects around – one to give the 'lesson' or description of the furnishings and one just to serve as security. You are, after all, borrowing your neighbor's most cherished physical possession, his home, and it's up to you and your members to make certain that there is absolutely no damage or thievery committed during the tour. Tickets for such tours usually start at $5, but often they are quite a bit more.

148 You can also have small boutique items for sale, providing there's space in one of the locations, and it fits in with the timing and flow of the tour itself. A boutique sales item for a children's room tour would be a Tooth Fairy pillow – lacy, frilly little pillows for girls and pillows with frogs, bandana prints, etc. for boys – with a tiny pocket for that lost tooth.

149 You might line up donors to pay for the printing of a nice program book telling the history of each home or garden and containing a few pictures. These, too, become collectors' items and sell well. One group, after approximately ten years of house tours, published a book which featured all the homes and which sold very well and made even more money for their organization.

150 Usually – well, a lot of the time – one stop along the tour will provide light refreshments for the visitors. Tea, wine and cheese, or cocktails would be appropriate. Ticket price will depend on what your expenses are for the day, and that includes the refreshments you'll be serving plus paper napkins, etc. If your tour highlights children's or teenagers' rooms, you might like to have refreshments suitable for each age group – bite size pizzas, cola, and the like for the teenagers and the ubiquitous chocolate chip cookie and something to sip for the children. But served elsewhere, of course.

8 Chef in Residence

With recipes for Unicorn Horns, Elephant Ears, Donuts, Rootbeer Floats, Rock Candy, Funny Cake, No-milk Cake, Fresh Horseradish; Watermelon Sold Easily; Sticks and Stones Cookery (including recipes for bacon-fruit-kabobs, jam twists and angel kisses); Bake Sales; Ice Cream Socials; Dime-a-dip Dinners; Survival Kits for College Kids; Cookbooks

Chef in Residence

If your group wants to sell what they make, and they are definitely not interested in making woven potholders, they have probably decided they want to cook. (I once thought I could never use up all those little potholders my eight-year-old made, but I wish now she'd go back into business!)

151 Your group could set up a booth at some event and sell their goodies across the counter piping hot from the stove. Piping hot also means you have a safety problem to deal with. So keep that in mind and make darned sure you have adults who know what they're doing on hand at all times during the preparation and sale of your piping-hots. A vat of bubbling hot grease spilled on anyone is not just a safety hazard, it is a tragedy, and one we can – must – do without.

The obvious hot food items you can sell are hot dogs, hamburgers, barbecues, and cozy-dogs. All of these have their spot in the history and nostalgia of our nation, but none of them is especially exciting.

152 Unicorns and elephants, on the other hand, are exciting. Your group can come up with hot UNICORN HORNS or ELEPHANT EARS almost as easily as falling off a log, if you do it the easy way. Remember that, in both cases, you're dealing with that dangerous hot grease. Both species come from the refrigerator shelves of your supermarket in the guise of poppin' fresh refrigerated doughs already mixed and stored in a neat, compact little tube. Yes, refrigerator biscuits and breads.

153 Elephant Ears will require a bread board, rolling pin and some extra flour and/or butter/margarine to make handling the dough easier. The individual biscuits are rolled out flat, using as little flour as possible, and then fried in a deep electric skillet of hot fat. After it is golden brown on both sides, drain it on paper towels, sprinkle generously with cinnamon-sugar and serve on another clean towel.

154 Unicorn Horns are a way to support the current craze for this legendary animal. Take a refrigerated biscuit, roll it between your palms (using butter or flour, whichever you feel works better) until you have formed it into a long, lean horn. Fry it in grease and dip one end (at least half its length) into a thin, white glaze or icing made from powdered sugar and milk. Again, you'll need paper towels for draining, napkins or towels for serving, and a fairly deep bowl or pan to keep your dipping glaze in.

155 You can also make fresh donuts using the above method. Cut the centers out with a regular donut cutter or the sharp edge of a small pill bottle. Fry the donuts in hot fat, drain, and dredge with powdered sugar, plain white sugar, brown sugar or cinnamon-sugar.

156 Another sure-fire seller on a hot day is WATERMELON. On July 4, 1976 our small C.A.R. watermelon booth cleared over four hundred dollars, and we learned the easy ways to handle this beautiful roly-poly ruby-centered emerald of the garden. We sliced the melon lengthwise and then into slices which resembled pie halves. It took two members to hold that rocking-chair melon and another to cut those half-pie wedges through. When the second shift showed up to work, a resourceful father took one look at our struggles (and our sore thumbs from holding that knife so hard), flipped the half-a-melon over on its ruby red face and started cutting through the rind first. Voilà! Easy. We kept paper napkins (lots of them) and salt handy, and served the melon slices on foil wrap sheets. Our melons were stored and displayed in a clean farm tank loaned by a farmer-father, with bags of ice keeping them cool. The previous night (since we had to pick them up a day early), they were stored in a dairy truck loaned to us by a friendly milk company. We were just using our resources. And we made enough to win a prize at the national Children of the American Revolution convention the following spring!

157 Fresh HORSERADISH is something fairly unique that your group might sell. It's especially fitting for an old-fashioned holiday or if you're taking part in a celebration at an historic site. And it's great if you've had the forethought to raise your own horseradish roots. Be sure to wash them first. For your sales effort you'll need pans of water, paring knives to peel the roots, grinders, and small jars in which to put the horseradish. (The grinders can be hand operated or electric, depending on what you have and whether you wish to remain 'old-fashioned'.) Baby food jars are excellent to put the horseradish in, so put out the word in plenty of time to all of your friends and neighbors to save their Beechnut and Gerber's jars for you. Needless to say, they have to be spotlessly clean! It's an added touch if you've painted the lids or made little cloth circles to tie over and around them. A warning: this is a hot item. Literally. Be sure the members working with it know they can get it into their eyes and be most uncomfortable for a while. There's no permanent damage, but beware, nevertheless.

158 ROOT BEER FLOATS are an excellent sales item for a Gay Nineties or Victorian theme, and tie in well with almost any Fourth of July celebration. You'll need vanilla ice cream, root beer, good sized paper or plastic cups or glasses, and straws and plastic spoons long enough to reach the bottom of the glass. Obviously, you'll have to find ways of keeping your ice cream cold. But when you purchase the ice cream from the dairy, they will no doubt be able to give you assistance in this matter, perhaps by loaning or renting you a cooler. If you're lucky enough to have a member with contacts in the dairy or refrigeration business, you have it made. You might want to go with more flavors – that decision is strictly up to you.

159 Something you may not see much, but which is relatively easy to sell and definitely unique, is ROCK CANDY. It looks like jewels and is sweet as sugar (because that's what it's made of). It makes a colorful display for your booth and is also quite a conversation piece. To make the candy, the basic recipe is simple. Pour a cup of water into a pan and add two cups of sugar. Stir this mixture over medium heat until the sugar is all melted. Keep adding more sugar, a cup at a time, and stir until the sugar will no longer dissolve in the water. Stop adding sugar when you can see it lying on the bottom of the pan. Remove the pan from the stove and let it cool until it is just warm, then pour it into a clean glass jar, preferably a quart size. Tie one end of a clean cord around a pencil or short piece of wood (the wooden handle of a rubber spatula is great because it won't roll) so the cord is almost as deep as the jar. Let the cord fall into the sugar water. In just a few hours, crystals will begin to form around the string. The following day, drain off the remaining liquid and reheat it. (Handle the cord and its crystals carefully – they can be left to dangle in the empty jar.) Cool the reheated liquid as you did before, then pour it back into the jar. More crystals will form. Do this for several days and your rock candy will grow like the proverbial Topsy. You can add coloring to each batch of sugar water and come up with some really exciting jewel colors. After the strings have grown a good inch of candy crystal around the cord, take them out and hang them to dry. Display your rock candy by hanging it in a bright light so your customers can see all the lovely colors of the rainbow you have just created.

160 Something else your members can make and sell on the spot are STICKS AND STONES. We call it that because it's cooked on sticks or skewers. You need charcoal grills for this, and someone to keep an eye on the endeavor, because charcoal-burning can be dangerous.

Do not – repeat – DO NOT use charcoal if you are working inside a building or enclosure because charcoal has a way of using up all the available oxygen in the air, and you can end up quite dead before you know it. Charcoal is a wonderful aid for heating and cooking, but it can also be deadly, and anyone using it should keep that in mind.

161 One thing you might make and cook on skewers is BACON-FRUIT KEBABS which are made by using quartered apples which are then cut in half, widthwise. Cut a banana into four thick slices and wrap a half piece of bacon around each. Fasten the bacon with a sharp twig or toothpick, thread two banana and two apple slices alternately on your stick or skewer. Grill over hot coals until the bacon is done.

Many ethnic-type fairs have lamb, pork or beef kebabs which are fairly easy to imitate. Just marinate your one-to-two inch chunks of meat (Did we mention chicken? That's good, too.) in a spicy-type salad dressing such as Italian, skewer the meat with or without such items as pineapple chunks, cherry tomatoes, mushrooms, etc., and you have a feast on a stick. For a less expensive version, you can use bulk (unsliced) luncheon meats (even bologna) cut into chunks, dipped into various sauces and cooked on skewers with pineapple and other goodies.

162 A second food item to cook on the grill is another use of refrigerated biscuits, this time just flattened and wrapped around a stick about an inch in diameter and cooked until it is golden brown. Load jam into a cookie press and fill your JAM TWISTS.

163 Another item is even easier. Use a loaf of day-old Italian or French bread and cut it into one-inch cubes. Skewer the cube, dip it in a can of sweetened condensed milk, let the excess milk drip off, and then roll it in flaked coconut. (If you want to cut down on the expense of buying sweetened condensed milk, use condensed cream or milk to which you have added light or dark syrup, or even flavored syrup like you serve on pancakes.) Toast until golden brown. One loaf of bread will make about 24 of these ANGEL KISSES.

164 Another obvious fundraiser for people who like to cook is a BAKE SALE. The first thing you need, of course, is the date and the place to hold your sale. A Saturday morning or day before a holiday seems to work best for all – customers and cooks. A local shopping mall is super, as everyone does their weekend shopping. Some small grocery stores which do not have their own bakery section will often let community groups set up shop on their premises. If you're so lucky, for gosh sakes, don't forget that thank-you letter afterwards.

165 A table, large enough to display your wares, covered with a clean, white paper or tablecloth (sheets come in handy) is a must. Also necessary are extra sacks and plastic or foil to cover any items which are brought in uncovered. Perhaps you might even have a small supply of paper plates, just in case two customers decide to share one purchase and split it in half on the spot. Use small flag-type price tags. These can be made with seals stuck back to back on a toothpick which is then stuck into the pie or cake without damaging it.

166 You may wish to include homemade jams and jellies when you're calling your members for donations, too. The best sellers are usually a super-high angel food cake with fluffy icing and – just take a whiff – homemade bread. If you have a bread baker in your midst, don't, for heaven's sake, let him or her get away. You have found a treasure.

167 You might want to just feature baked goods or other food items which have no preservatives in them or foods for diabetics or other people with certain dietary needs – go to the library if you need recipes. Be sure to advertise this well in advance so those you're targeting as customers will show up. You'd be surprised how leery 'regular' customers can be of a cake which is advertised as having no milk, eggs, or sugar.

168 If you want a good recipe for a chocolate cake with no eggs, you might want to try the FUNNY CAKE which was a 4-H Club show recipe for years. Put 1½ cups flour, 1 cup sugar, ¼ cup cocoa powder, and 1 teaspoon soda into an ungreased 8" x 8" x 2" cake pan. With your mixing spoon, make three holes in the dry mixture in the pan. Into one hole put 1 teaspoon vinegar, into the second put 1 teaspoon vanilla, and into the last hole pour ⅓ cup oil or melted fat and ½ teaspoon salt. Pour 1 cup cold water gradually over the mixture in the pan and stir until there are no lumps. Be sure to get the corners mixed in, too, and spread the mixture well and evenly over the bottom of the pan. Bake about 35 minutes in a pre-heated (350° F) oven until the cake pulls away slightly from the edge of the pan. Let the cake cool and then frost it (although it's so good, you may not want to wait to frost it). How about that? No pans to wash!

169 A NO MILK CAKE that is probably as good as anything you've ever put into your mouth is baked in an angel food cake pan or a bundt pan with a center tube, for about an hour and twenty minutes at 350°. It has 3 cups of flour, 1 teaspoon of baking soda, 1 teaspoon cinnamon, 2 cups sugar, 1 teaspoon salt, 1¼ cups cooking oil, one 8-ounce can of crushed pineapple with juice; 1½ teaspoons of vanilla, 3 eggs, 2 cups of ripe bananas and 1 cup of pecan pieces. The dry ingredients are mixed together, and then the fruit, nuts, eggs, oil, and vanilla are added and stirred until blended. Do not beat.

That trip to the recipe section of your library can give you countless other excellent and easy recipes which you can use for your specialty bake sale or in your own kitchen for your own family.

170 Something that's nice to have at a bake sale is a good supply of pretty little recipe cards and the plastic envelopes in which they fit to keep them clean. (These can be ordered from the Current Company listed in our Party-Party and Door-To-Door chapter.) You might also sell your special recipes which you've neatly typed or printed on pretty recipe cards. If the recipes are original, you can sell them for quite a bit – sometimes even a dollar each. But if you're copying from a cookbook, they should sell for less and should credit the book they came from. Check copyright laws on this.

171 Another fundraiser which finds you and your members serving food to the public is the old-fashioned ICE CREAM SOCIAL. Ever since that ancient Roman (or whoever else it was) discovered ice cream, there have probably been ice cream socials. This is a summertime event and you will need to line up homemade cakes to serve with the ice cream. You'll also need at least three flavors of ice cream – vanilla, chocolate and strawberry seem to be the favorites. Again, consult with your dairy which supplies the ice cream to make sure it is packed so it won't melt in the heat of the summer afternoon or evening. Often the price of the ice cream includes small paper plates, paper napkins and plastic spoons. (I'm old enough that I can remember those lovely small wooden spoons – absolutely flat – which I delighted in digging into that scrumptious ice cream – and which are now collector's items!) But be sure to check it out. You may have to purchase these items yourself.

172 The afternoon or evening of the social you will have to have tables and chairs set up where your customers can sit and enjoy their refreshments. You'll also need plenty of helpers to make sure the tables are kept spotless. Remember, summer is a time of insects and especially that pesky fly, so you don't want those critters crawling all over the tables, spoiling the spirit of the occasion. Having warm, soapy water to sponge off the tables will greatly help – cold rinse water simply isn't good enough for that problem.

173 Be prepared for some people who will want to trade in their tickets (sold ahead of time, naturally, to give you some idea of how many to plan for) for plates of cake and ice cream to take out. You will need something a little sturdier than the small cake plate for these customers.

Sometimes placing the scoops of ice cream in paper cups is the best way to handle the 'take-outs' and you can still use the small paper plates for the cake. You should also have something for your customers to drink – iced tea, coffee, lemonade, or ice water served in paper or styrofoam cups.

174 Another way of selling food to the public, of course, is THE DINNER, THE SUPPER or even THE BREAKFAST. This could be a TURKEY DINNER, a CHILI SUPPER, or a PANCAKE and SAUSAGE BREAKFAST, with which you're all familiar. Or you could go for something different like a DIME-A-DIP DINNER. This is a way to raise funds and also get a lot of attention for your group and laughter for all. You might want to hold it just within your own organization or open it to the public. Your members will provide the food, either a little for themselves, or in quantities if you've sold tickets to the public. The idea is that you sell the food for 10 cents a serving (you may want to up the price). You can have a small potluck for your own group and charge strictly 10 cents (or the determined price) per portion. Or you can sell tickets which entitle the customer to a certain specified number of servings, which will give you some idea of how many to plan for. It also gives you a guarantee of so many dollars up front.

175 The gimmick is to have lots and lots of varieties to choose from, so that each customer tries more servings than are guaranteed in the ticket price, thus increasing your intake of funds. No half-portions, either, at the serving table because that defeats your purpose and also slows down your serving line tremendously. If the ticket purchaser takes two salads, mashed potatoes, gravy, two meats, two vegetables, rolls and butter and a cup of coffee, that's 10 items, and he hasn't even gotten to his favorite – the dessert table – yet. Keep the servings fairly small, too, but not too small. With today's food prices, you probably will want to sell your food for more than a dime. But if it's all donated by local merchants or your members (somehow members are expected to donate so much), then you can keep it pretty low and still make a considerable amount. It's lots of fun, regardless.

Here again, you can add to your proceeds by having your members make up recipe cards for the dish they brought. The recipes are then sold.

176 Quite obviously, your 10-year-old Girl Campers can't do all this cooking, and you and all the other senior leaders and parents will be doing much – no, most – of that. But those cute little 10-year-olds can pull their own weight (and even more) in helping to serve, helping senior citizens carry their plates to the tables, clearing the table, refilling water glasses and the like. It's their organization, after all, and they don't expect you to do it all. Besides, they're super help, and this is how little girls and boys learn to later be adult leaders of children's organizations. Another lesson hidden in doing something that's fun.

177 Two more super great ideas for raising funds which require a bit of time in the kitchen (a lot of which can be spent by those 10-year-olds, by the way) are the fairly new concepts of the SURVIVAL KIT for college students during finals week and the BIRTHDAY CAKE for college students or military people away from home.

These require prior clearance from college and military base officials, if you want easy access to their lists of names. Otherwise, because you'll be contacting, in most cases, the parents of the students and young sailors and soldiers, you will have a hard time getting the right names and addresses. In the town where my daughter attends Illinois State University, parents of the students receive a form letter in the fall, about a month prior to first semester exams, which offers, for $4, a Survival Kit to be sent in December, and for another four bucks, a second one in May. The kit contains such goodies as homemade chocolate chip cookies, cracker and cheese packs, fresh fruit, beef jerky sticks, gum, candy, and the like.

178 The same address lists can be used for providing birthday cakes for college students, although this slows down as a going business during the summer months when few students are on campus. It is something you can use all year long in your own town, though, if you advertise that you will deliver birthday (or anniversary, or . . .) cakes to people at their office or home. I've seen some really interesting cakes – some resembling Dolly Parton's torso – delivered to business executives at their office.

179 Birthday cakes to military personnel are a really heart-warming endeavor. If there are prohibitions against receiving the names and addresses of the soldiers' parents, you can probably get permission to display posters which the men and women in uniform see. This poster should list the address of your operation, so they can send you their parents' addresses and the parents can 'hint' what their loved one would like for his special day. Anytime you're mailing to the parents, you're talking about the expense of printing letters or brochures (they don't have to be fancy) and postage. You can either bake cakes in your own kitchens, or get them from commercial bakeries. Your services are priced accordingly. As a special, you might have some young military personnel over for a home-cooked meal and a birthday cake. That won't make you any money, except what the parents paid for the cake, but it sure makes you feel good.

180 Another way to make money from your kitchens is to publish your own COOKBOOK. Admittedly, this is a long-range project, and will take some work on behalf of your members. They must collect the recipes, edit them, put them into order, make up a good index and get the cookbook printed and distributed. (You'll get at least ten recipes exactly the same. If you will be listing the contributor's names, it may take one page for just one recipe. You don't want to waste space, which you will be paying for, by printing the same recipe over and over again. If there are slight variations, they should be shown as such, so again, you aren't listing 'practically' the same recipe over and over again. And if you're listing the names of the contributors, leaving any of them out will result in hurt feelings or worse.)

181 How much you pay the printer is determined by how much work you are willing to do. If you take it to him camera-ready, the cost will be less. If you let him do all the scratching and scrabbling, the costs go up. (Though there aren't many printers anymore who will even bother. There are editing firms who will do it for a price, naturally.) What kind of binding you choose affects the price you will need to charge for your cookbook. Get bids from various printers – it's worth the additional time it will take to do so, and they will have many worthwhile pointers for you.

182 One of the bindings which will let the pages of your book fall open is the plastic spiral. But try to make certain it isn't the cheap kind which pops open every time you use it and lets the pages fall helter-skelter on the kitchen floor. A hardback book will be most expensive. If you go that route, be sure it's bound so it will stay open to the recipe you're using. No one wants a cookbook that snaps shut like a clothespin every time you set it down.

You might think you can get by with a Xeroxed, stapled version and save money, but it will pay you to go to a more expensive publication. Not only will it sell better, it will last better, and you'll be much prouder to have the name of your organization on its frontispiece.

9 Services, Seminars and Simpleton-simple Ideas

Good Deeds for Older Citizens; House-sitting, Babysitting, Pet Care, Survival Kits, Catering, Tours, a Variety of Seminars, Other Novelty Services

Services, Seminars and Simpleton-simple Ideas

Your organization can increase the balance of its savings account by just looking around your neighborhood (one of your resources, remember?) and seeing what kinds of services are needed or might be welcomed from time to time.

183 If you have a goodly supply of older residents, there are many ways in which your young people can perform good deeds and receive a bit of remuneration in return. Offering to help our older neighbors for nothing is, in their eyes, charity. So they will be retaining their self-respect when they avail themselves of your services and you permit them to reimburse you. Many times you would have enjoyed helping them for nothing.

184 Perhaps they need transportation. Advances in modern medicine mean that many oldsters are still pretty spry and like to do their own shopping. But because of the unavailability of public transportation, or its relative lack of safety, they remain caged in their own homes, yearning to get out and do their own things.

You and your older, responsible driving members can take them to the grocery store, club meeting, movie, medical appointments or all those other places they're missing so much. You might also offer to take their pets to the veterinary. (Be sure to put the pet on a leash and/or in a wire cage for transportation, especially if you're going alone.)

185 They might even prefer to stay home and let you do their grocery shopping (with their list and funds). Or they might like to have a party and let you transport their no-driving guests to and from the party. Many of them may have arthritic limbs and need help addressing their Christmas cards or wrapping their gifts. If they live in their own homes, almost always they will need such services as lawns mowed, snow shovelled, and help with putting up and taking down storm windows and screens.

186 Sometimes you may know that your older citizens do not have the funds to pay your youngsters for their help, and yet may desperately need the help they are too proud to ask for. Why not barter with them? Perform needed services for them, and in return have them teach your youngsters such skills as knitting, tatting, crocheting, quilting, and many other crafts. These, in turn, can be put to good use in making items for sale at bazaars and other fundraisers you may have where you need pretty things to sell. There may be an initial period where no money comes into the club's coffers as you and your older neighbors pool and share your talents and skills. But those skills are worth their weight, literally, in gold for your organization as well as the overall growth and education of your young people.

187 Another service might be house-sitting for neighbors on vacation. This could include, if you have older members, actual on-site living, or just a daily visitation and checking of the premises to make sure the doors are locked, the mail is deposited safely inside, the flowers are watered, and different lights are left on throughout the house, as the time goes by, to discourage would-be housebreakers.

188 Young working mothers might be very appreciative of having responsible teen-agers pick up their children after school or kindergarten, escort them home, and take care of them until mother returns from work.

189 Pet owners may need various services performed for them and their beloved pets. You could take them to the vet (don't forget the part about the leash and/or cage), walk them, or bathe them. To wash a good-sized dog, you'll need two tubs – one to wash and one to rinse – and two workers – one to wash and one to hold the pet. A muzzle is a good idea if the mutt hates to take a bath. You might hold a public Pet Wash (as you would a Car Wash) on a nice summer day, letting everyone bring their pets to be shampooed. If you can get some flea collars, fancy bottles of shampoo, and other pet needs from a dealer on consignment, you could sell such supplies to the pet owners at the same time. If you don't buy regular pet shampoos for your Pet Wash project, at least buy no-tear baby shampoo for washing around their face and eyes. Flea shampoos should be used for those pets with fleas, starting at the neck (use no-tear stuff on the head) and working toward the tail, so the fleas can take their leave just ahead of the suds. Flea shampoos are very strong and should never be used around the dog's eyes or nose.

190 If you're in the Dog Jogging business as a fundraiser, check with your local officials and see what the ordinances are concerning pets out on the sidewalks and streets. Is a leash required? Muzzle? Where can you NOT go? You should carry some means to dispose of anything the pet deposits during your walk, and make sure the deposit is not done on anyone's lawn. Your own pooper-scooper and a plastic bag should be standard equipment. The used bag can be deposited in the trash can nearest the pet's residence. Be sure not to dispose of it too quickly as you might need it a second time on one route. For caring for pets, you should charge approximately the same rate as is normal for babysitting in your area. Practice all these on your family dog.

191 Speaking of babysitting, one way of raising funds in your neighborhood might be to publish a Babysitting Area Babysitting Directory. It would contain not only babysitting and child care hints, but also the names of babysitters, which ages they prefer to care for, what their hourly rate is, and their telephone number. The babysitter pays $1 to have his or her name included on the list. The families purchasing the book also pay a small fee to have their own copy of potential sitters. The price they pay depends on how much the printing costs are and whether the book you publish contains advertisements of local merchants who deal in children's merchandise. If you go for a home-printing job, the book sells for less and does not contain the advertisements. You can upgrade the book by having tear-out pages which are used by the parent on each occasion they have a babysitter. On this page the parents list where they will be for that particular day or night (in case of emergency), what the child's favorite foods and toys are, any medical problems which might pop up, and emergency telephone numbers for fire, police and ambulance.

192 One such directory charged $10 to merchants for a 2½" x 2½" box ad in the book, and sold to families for under $2.50. The organization realized a profit of around $2 per book in a printing of five hundred copies. Posters advertising the directory were put up in various locations and there was minimum advertising in a local paper. As with any venture dealing with unknown patrons, try to remind both babysitters and parents to obtain references from the people they hire or for whom they work. There are always kooks looking for a place to create havoc, and taking precautions is the name of the game if we are to avoid tragedy.

193 Another service which is somewhat on a par with the Survival Kit and Birthday Cake deliveries, is a service for divorced fathers. It helps them remember the birthdays and major events in the lives of their far-away children, by signing them up to a subscription service where your group remembers to purchase and send appropriate gifts at appropriate times. Some of us may think this is a rather impersonal way to remember the separated children, but divorce and separation of families is a devastating situation and has to be handled in different ways by different people. It may seem impersonal on the part of the father – to let someone else do his shopping and mailing of birthday gifts – but it is very personal at the other end, when a child, lonely for his missing parent, receives a package at just the right time.

194 The initial step in such a procedure is to advertise. Then the subscribers fill out a form which gives the names, ages, birthdates, likes and dislikes, and other special dates and pertinent information about the children. The father also indicates the amount of money he wishes to spend in a given year (perhaps a minimum of thirty-five dollars would be your starting point). You then accept his check, give him a copy of his subscription-contract, and make sure his children get their gifts. Here is another time it is helpful to have a lawyer within your ranks.

195 Other services for which many people are more than willing to pay are having you take their children to the zoo (be sure you have a sufficient number of helpers if you're going to be chasing kids all day), writing their Christmas cards for them (great if you have members with good handwriting or a script typewriter), and decorating their lawn (and/or cleaning it first) for an outside party, or their offices for Christmas. (There are professional firms who do this all the time. You can probably offer a better price because you have free labor and all you have to buy is the decorating material which the office pays for.)

196 You might offer to cater a business breakfast for a local firm. If they have to go to a restaurant, they are surrounded by all the other customers, but you can offer them a great deal of privacy if you serve it in the church dining room, for instance, or even in their own building on rented tables and chairs. Breakfast menus offer great potential for such fundraising, and it's something different the business can offer its sales staff or customers brought in for a special seminar or meeting of some kind. Distribute Xeroxed brochures among your business community, and rake in the money for your new ballclub uniforms.

197 You might arrange tours for children, adults, or foreign visitors, and take them sight-seeing to farms, factories, parks, theatres, ballgames, even garage sales, or any other interesting spots in your vicinity. You would arrange the transportation either member-driven or chartered buses, make reservations or other arrangements for meals, collect the ticket money, and grab a seat on the bus to go along and see everyone else enjoying themselves.

198 If there is absolutely nowhere in your community which lends itself to a tour, throw a "Let's Pretend Tour", and sell tickets. You don't even have to supply the transportation for this one, just the location. When your customers arrive for their tour, they will find themselves in some exotic, real or make-believe land, where the decorations, foods, entertainment and favors all are flavored with seasoning of foreign lands or the imagination of some author. You can transport your guests to the South Seas, the Orient, the Far East, Old England, France, Scandinavia, Never-Never Land, The Land of the Lilliputians, or wherever some current movie or book may give you "free tickets", i.e. a theme idea. If you're traveling to a real location, find some interesting movies you can show to get everyone in the mood. Have a showing of the movie ahead of time for you and your committee – you'll get lots of ideas to carry out your theme.

199 If you go through the yellow pages of your phone book you will probably think of all sorts of services which your group could duplicate and at a lesser price than the professional. This gives your customers a chance to benefit from the lower price and your organization a chance to raise funds. Don't take on more than you can handle, though. "Know your resources" means know how much time you and the others can contribute to the project, all the various angles which have to be considered, and make sure you do a quality job of whatever you do.

200 Another important aspect of knowing your resources is to recognize all the talent you have floating around in your group and within their immediate families. Many relatives would be willing to contribute their talents rather than actual funds, and you can benefit as a result.

201 You might, if you have appropriate locations, offer seminars in woodworking (something many of our older relatives are quite proficient at and would interest the younger set a great deal) or fitness. Make up your own health club, sell lots of memberships to neighbors who couldn't otherwise afford the expensive fancy clubs, and get everyone trim and fit, bending and stretching to the rhythm of one-two-three, or whatever it takes to trim an inch or two off waist or thigh. Having someone in your group who's trained in this type of activity is preferred, or you could hire a school coach and pay him or her a percentage of the fee your subscribers pay. Collect the subscription fee in advance. If your customers have already paid their fees, they will be less apt to drop out. Should they drop out, anyway, you already have their money (you held a space for them, so you deserve it) and that's good for you and your organization.

202 Do you have a writer in your group? Or a genealogist? These are two fields many people are interested in, yet they are hesitant to sign up for expensive classes at the local university. If you have teachers willing to donate their expertise (or take a token payment), you can charge a fair rate for your series of workshops – anywhere from two to a dozen would be appropriate – and everyone can benefit. If you don't have a writer in your group, contact your local college and see if they can suggest someone working on his master's degree who would be willing to help you and gain experience for himself.

If you don't have anyone in your group who knows anything about climbing trees, let alone checking family trees, contact your nearest chapter of the D.A.R. – Daughters of the American Revolution – for help in conducting your seminar. Their chapters get credit from the national organization for doing such work. Your organization can benefit from the expertise. It would be appropriate to offer an honorarium to a D.A.R. chapter or a part of the seminar enrollment proceeds to the D.A.R. member and chapter who give you such assistance.

203 If you have someone proficient in a foreign language, or some aspect of foreign food preparation, see if you can't promote a seminar to share such talents. Tennis, swimming, crafts of all sorts – these are the sorts of talents you can share with others and make a profit for your organization as you do so.

204 Whenever you are selling things that will be used for gifts, offer a GIFT-WRAPPING SERVICE. At Christmas time, you might see if you could get permission to set up your own gift-wrap business inside the local shopping mall.

205 You might sell Gift Certificates for all sorts of things, to any of the services listed above, or, in addition, for such fun things as Breakfast in Bed or other hot meals served at a specific time to a specific person. College sororities and fraternities make a buck or two having "Tuck-Ins", where they take subscriptions to go "tuck-in" another student (usually of the opposite sex) at the dorm complete with appropriate lullaby, huggable toy and sometimes a bedtime snack. A photographer goes along to record the event for student and subscriber, usually parents.

206 Other services are fun-oriented. Western Union has, for a long time, offered singing telegrams. They went out of that particular phase of their business for a while, but have gone back into it again. Other commercial organizations offer Balloon-O-Gram, Cookie-O-Gram, and all sorts of surprise birthday celebration gimmicks. Your organization can reap some benefits from such ventures if you have outgoing members willing to deliver the balloons in December, dressed in their bikinis, for instance, or willing to deliver a cake, while dressed in a clown outfit. (That shouldn't take too much stamina.) Come up with some ideas of your own. The first step is to decide what you can do. The second is to advertise and get the word around. It doesn't have to be commercial advertising, as we've already discussed in an earlier chapter.

207 You might have a seminar in the proper use of make-up. This would be something both teenagers and older women would enjoy. A deal could be worked out with a commercial line of cosmetics to share in the sale of the cosmetics after the demonstration. Or just sell tickets in advance and pay the demonstrator (if you don't have one in your ranks) a flat fee.

208 Do you have an artist? Make reservations for pastel portraits, or whatever type of personal artistics he or she might have to offer, and share the profits. You do the advertising, set up the appointments, and the artist does the work. You might take orders for oil paintings done from colored photos, instead of 'settings'. These can be done as 'surprise' gifts – which you can stress in your advertising – and give the artist more time to accomplish the job.

209 Some organizations even use eggs to raise money. But I can't tell you about that yet. Instead, how about setting up a day camp for children during the summer? Line up the families who will share the 'camp duty', holding it at their homes for one day. Also, line up the helpers, decide on what will be offered to the campers, sell subscriptions (registration fee plus hourly fee, in advance), and, if necessary, provide transportation. You might decide to hold it only Monday-Wednesday-Friday or all five days. It might be a Saturday-only thing. Be sure to have your lawyer pal draw up a simple contract for this project, and check out your liability insurance. Leonard Lawyer will know what to tell you. What would we do without our friendly lender of legal advice?

210 Another rather silly little service which can reap the benefits for your group is to advertise (assuming you have a resident poet of sorts) that you will deliver a poem upon request and payment of an appropriate fee. The purchaser will supply you with the pertinent information about the recipient of the gift poem, and you go from there. Your price should include a nice grade of paper for the printing of the poem, an appropriate frame, and, if possible, some pretty lettering or calligraphy of the words. Don't forget to add any expenses you might incur in delivering the poem, especially if it has to be mailed. You might call this project Terse Verse. Or you might think of a name better. Or even Worse.

211 Another service you might offer is a child's birthday party complete with decorations, entertainment, favors and refreshments. Audio and video recordings of the event would be an added option, if you have the capabilities. Kids love clowns, cowboys and Indians, and comic book heroes, heroines and monsters. So the ideas for your parties are copious, if you've any imagination at all. (And, obviously, if you are working with kids in the first place, you need a lot of that – if only so you can imagine you're home, soaking in a tub of bubbles or reading your favorite sexy novel, instead of standing in the freezing cold, collecting tickets to the ice skating party your group is sponsoring tonight, or . . .)

212 Or you might offer to tape Christmas greetings (or any other time, too) for people to send to their friends and relatives who live miles away. All it takes is a good cassette recorder, a blank tape, and a bit of PR to let folks know you're ready, willing and able to put their words, if not on marble, at least on tape. Charge according to the price of the tape (but use good ones) and your time. The 'time' money goes into the club treasury, the tape expense is reimbursed.

213

Something that isn't basically a service, but renders aid in several directions, is to collect toys, fix those which need to be fixed, and sell them to raise money for your cause. Or, if your group needs a 'credit' for good deeds on their state or national honor roll, give the toys to underprivileged children.

214

Another service you might offer is a Coupon Book which offers free or discount items from local merchants who sign a contract with your organization agreeing to honor the coupons when presented. This will take several months to line up donors and get the book printed and sold. But it is an outstanding money maker for any group, as long as it's carefully done, and you deal only with merchants you know to be reputable and willing to live up to the obligations of the coupon book. You will have a substantial bill for printing up-front, so bear that in mind. Use a contract.

215

You can offer another service to your community by picking up litter – and profit from selling the trash – especially if it's aluminum beer or soda cans. You can help clear your neighbors' back porches and basements of old newspapers, and, even if your local scrap paper business isn't, convert them to dollars.

216 How to convert old newspapers to dollars? Easy. Turn them into logs for the fireplace at prices lots cheaper than real logs or those authentic jobs they have at the grocery store. In a large tub, mix water and detergent (enough to make the water feel 'soft'). Fold some newspapers into a stack about one and one-half inches thick, and place these in the tub until the paper is soaked. Then take the paper out and roll it around the end of a broom or a similar heavy stick. You can also buy a gadget which is supposed to speed up this process and doesn't cost much. Press and squeeze out the excess water as you roll the paper. Add a second layer. When the log is as thick as you desire, pull out the wooden roller and let the log dry. The drying will take at least a couple of days although a week is better. Put it in a warm, dry place to store. Don't try selling any of the logs until you've tried them in your own fireplace to make sure they've dried enough and are approximately the right size. They usually burn very well because the hole in the middle, left by the roller, gets the heat into the very center of the log. You can charge at least fifty cents for each log. Compare it with the price of firewood in your community and go accordingly. Start this project in the fall so you have a good supply ready for sale when the first nip sets in and people start enjoying their fireplaces. You can fancy-up your logs by covering them with wood-pattern wallpaper samples.

217 What's my definition of something that is "Simpleton – Simple" when it comes to raising funds? I offer A Mile of Pennies. A church I know of decided it needed an easy (though not super quick) way to raise funds for a given project. Knowing that everyone usually has those little brown round pennies in their pocket most of the time, they latched on to the idea of a mile of pennies. For your edification, a mile of pennies measured 5,280 feet, and is made up of 84,480 pennies, or $844.80 cash value. This project does best if there are weekly bulletins put out somehow to let all the members know how close they are to their goal.

And the super easy one – of all easy ones – is The Egg. To be continued. (It's worth waiting for.)

10 Meeting Maneuvers and Talent On the Hoof

Bakeless Bake Sale; Pay by the Inch; Silent Auction, Second-hand-Rose Style Show; Doll Boutique; Tree Decorations From Real Green Stuff; Label Redemption; Cents-off Refunding; Kitchen Bands; Madrigal Singers

Meeting Maneuvers and Talent On the Hoof

218 Some groups just don't like bake sales, but are willing to make their contribution via a BAKE-LESS BAKE SALE. In a world of busy men and women, sometimes it's difficult to come up with enough freshly baked goodies to have a bake sale at your local mall or community fair. By announcing to your membership that you are saving them from having to spend a morning over a hot stove and messing up their kitchen, you can usually inspire them to grab their purse or checkbook and make their contribution directly to the group. There are actually several advantages to this method: one, you don't have to do the actual baking; two, you don't have to attend the bake sale and buy someone else's baked goods, and three, you have a check to show the IRS that you made a contribution to this charitable cause. Another great thing about a bakeless bake sale is that there are no calories!

219 Send out your Bakeless Bake Sale announcement letter (or deliver it to the members at your next meeting, thus saving postage) about six weeks ahead of the date you'd like your funds to all be 'in'. Put a deadline on the letter, by the way. Otherwise it can get lost at the back or bottom of the bills drawer, and you'll only waste your twenty cents postage.

220 Have someone in your group, who is handy with a poem, come up with the special wording of the announcement. Somehow a rhyme seems to bring in more money for your cause than will just a request for the money. If you don't have a resident poet, you might say, for instance:

BAKELESS BAKE SALE

You haven't time to bake?
Yes, we know how much time it takes,
so all we're asking of you, our member
is the cost of something sweet and tender
straight from your oven.
A cake, cookies, quick breads, ever-lovin'
special apple pie, or perhaps your fudge candy;
anything you send will be just dandy.
It will fill our coffers with lots of funds
to help the ___________, so forget the buns,
the cakes and cookies, too,
and get out your checkbook, send it to

_______________________________________.

Be sure we have your gift by ___ date,
we're working toward ____, so don't be late.
P.S. It's tax-deductible.

Of course, you can make your own, or change the above to suit your purposes, but this will give you some idea of what to shoot for.

221 Another fun way to get your members (especially if they're adults) to open their pocketbooks for the good of the order, is to have a "Pay-By-The-Inch" fundraiser. You decide what the increment is, in dollars or cents, and charge by the size of the member's waist. You should also have a good-sized

amount which can be paid by those members who do not want the size of their waist divulged, whatever the cause! At ten cents an inch, my 32'er would be worth $3.20, but I just might be willing to pay $5 to keep everyone from finding out!

222 Another good fundraiser which can easily be held in conjunction with your regular meeting, is a SILENT AUCTION. Members bring in items which are displayed. Everyone then puts his name and bid on paper, under or in the same box as the item he's bidding on. The item goes to the highest bidder at the end of the auction. You might line up donations from local merchants (bless their hearts) if you want to have a really super night of high bidding.

223 You might also have members contribute good, but discarded, clothing which is in sizes that more than one member can wear. You wear this clothing to the meeting, where it is auctioned off to someone who admires it (and fits it], and the money is put into the club coffers. Hopefully, you won't forget to bring along a second outfit to wear home! This event is good for dozens of laughs. Be sure you're offering good quality items for auction – no one wants junk. You could bring something that was a gift, but is in a color which doesn't look best on you. Don't show up wearing something that looks absolutely rotten on you, though. If it looks that bad, no one will bid on it, even if it's mink! This is a SECOND-HAND-ROSE STYLE SHOW.

224 Something else that can begin at your regular meeting as a fundraiser is a DOLL BOUTIQUE. Ask everyone to bring one or more dolls to a meeting. All the dolls will probably need a new dress or outfit. The members can then take them home to redo them and bring them back at another prearranged meeting. Good public relations can be built around this project if you arrange to have the dolls displayed in a public building where they could be sold via an auction or silent auction. The proceeds can then go to your charitable project. The project can also be used as strictly a Christmas gift offering to underprivileged children. But that does not put money in your bank account – only warmth in your hearts.

225 Another fund-raiser which can be conducted at your club meeting is the raising of a Christmas Money Tree. Each member can make a decoration with a dollar bill (or even larger denominations). For instance, the wings of a bird could be the pleated green of a dollar bill. The dollar bill ornaments are then put on the hostess' tree for the evening. Afterwards, they are taken apart and become the proceeds for your treasury. Be sure to take pictures of some of the nifty ornaments your members are sure to come up with.

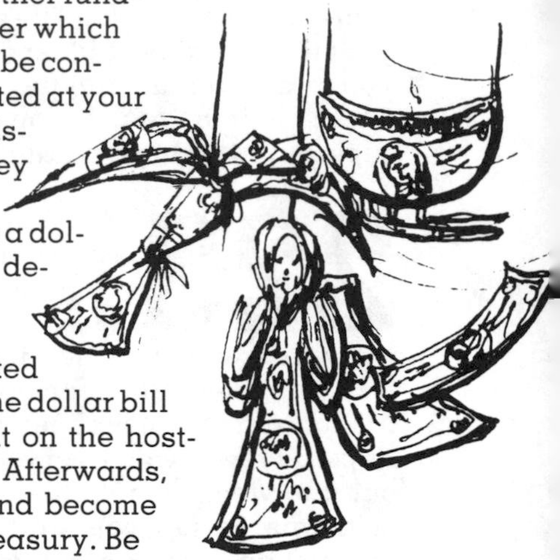

226 Another project which your members can do as they come to each meeting is collecting and donating various types of labels and/or coupons with national merchandising tie-ins. This can raise funds in large amounts. The Campbell Soup brand labels are used in one such project. Many schools, as well as the National Societies of Daughters (and Children) of the American Revolution, collect these labels for school projects. The DAR/CAR projects are connected with donations to the Bacone School for Indians in Muskogee, Oklahoma, and the St. Mary's School for Indian Girls in Springfield, South Dakota. Communication must be made with the food company to obtain specific rules for use of these proofs of purchase.

227 Other opportunities to obtain merchandise (which can then be resold) or cash refunds, are available on the bulletin boards of your local supermarket. Look them over. If you spy a cash refund you can obtain for a product you purchase all the time, tear off the little rebate/refund sheet and follow the directions. If all your members do the same, you can come up with a tidy little amount of cash added to your treasury balance. Books of Sperry and Hutchison (green) stamps also have a cash value, as do those of other trading stamp firms. Pool your resources (all those tiny single stamps in the bottom of your purses or drawers), cash them in and help the cause.

228 Talent on the hoof sounds theatrical, and that's what we mean. If you organized a kitchen band for some entertainment purpose for one of your meetings, put its members to work raising funds for the group now. If you came up with a beautifully costumed madrigal singing group for one of your December meetings, let them go professional – at least professional enough to put the word out they're available for other groups' Christmas programs, for nursing homes and the like. You can either charge a flat fee for your services, take up a freewill offering, or, in the spirit of the holiday, do it for nothing for those who can't afford to pay. You may not be collecting funds for charity, but you are performing a charitable act . . . and a loving act.

11 Hang Your Hat On a Holiday!

Halloween: Haunted House, Costume Rental, Costume Party; New Year's Eve; Twelfth Night; Lincoln and Washington's Birthdays; Valentine's Day; St. Patrick's Day (recipes for beer bread and fake scones); April Fools' Day; May Day; Independence Day; Friday, the Thirteenth

Hang Your Hat On a Holiday!

Holidays offer a multitude of opportunies for raising funds for your organization. Take advantage of them. Some examples of how you can just plain exploit holidays are listed below.

HALLOWEEN

229 HAUNTED HOUSE: This is not an easy project, but it is certainly a fun project. The first thing you need is a place to convert to a haunted house. If you're lucky enough to have a spooky-looking house in the neighborhood you can use, you're off and running. Of course, as with all projects, *be sure there are no safety hazards* to deal with which could create physical or financial havoc.

You will be dealing with many people at the same time, so the first things to plan for are easy, safe ways of ingress and exit. Then you start planning where you will place your spooks and goblins for optimum effect. Often a group will have a very simple Haunted House its first year out, and then build each year until it has reached an almost professional status when it comes to scary things to reach out and spook the paying guests. I recommend the slow start.

To begin with, old sheets, false faces, dark robes and weird noises can provide a lot of fright, when featured with flashing lights and more eerie sounds (pre-recorded on a tape recorder). The use of corpses rising from a coffin or actual skeletons suddenly walking beside a guest are things which can be worked out as the group's acumen improves.

230 If you know of a group in another town which has a Haunted House, talk to its members, and get some ideas. As long as you're not in actual competition with their efforts, you'll find they are generally cooperative in helping you come up with the spookiest possible Haunted House.

231 You should perhaps provide a daylight time to take small children through, when all the special effects are not in full force, so they can enjoy the spookhouse without being scared back into diapers. This teaches them – and visual aids are most effective – that Halloween and its spooks and goblins are just fun ways to celebrate a holiday. Many parents have found it useful in teaching their children not to be afraid of the dark or of strange sounds or things that go bump in the night.

232 If you don't have an actual house to use, basements or other rooms of schools, churches or community buildings can be turned into a pretty effective substitute. Use a maze-type approach which leads the ticket buyers through the spooky hauntings of the evening. Witches with their brooms can be part of the scary part, or you might use a friendly witch to lead the children through the maze. If you don't have enough walls in your room, turn long tables (like those in the school cafeteria) on end (making sure they're well supported) and create your own walls. Room dividers can also be made from folding screens and the like. Again, be sure at all times that you are offering your guests a safe evening of fun.

233 Don't use a scary idea if there is any chance of harming someone physically. Ditto for the house/room itself. It just isn't worth it. You may have some members – especially your older boys – who will have to be talked out of some of their more far-out ideas. In a year or two they may even have outgrown such ideas (but don't count on it!). By all means avoid all flammable materials. Candles in dark rooms are dangerous. They can easily be knocked over by those persons stumbling about in the darkness. Spooky gauzes, sheets and cardboard figures catch fire easily, and a spookhouse can quickly become a fire trap.

234 You might like to have a bake sale at the end of your tour where persons could purchase Halloween candy or homemade cupcakes iced in bright orange, for instance. Or cookies in the shape of Halloween cats, witches or pupkins. And don't forget pumpkin pie.

Decorate with a shock or two of corn and bright pumpkins, especially at lamp posts or just outside the door. If you need a ghost to float through the air, see Chapter 4. You can use any size of styrofoam ball, dowel and white cloth, for whatever size ghost you need. No need to hem the sheet – cut it evenly or pink with your pinking shears. Ghosts –

as with most spooks – do not haunt couturiers, at least not in the Halloween sense. A ghost floating eerily in the darkness is most effective.

235 The dime stores (if there are still such places) are full of Halloween decorations if you don't have ideas of your own. They usually aren't too expensive, but your members' families' closets are probably full of Halloween stuff they haven't used for years (unless you've already sold it at your group's garage sale) which they will be glad to donate to the cause. Don't forget – use your resources! It's cheaper, too.

236 HALLOWEEN COSTUME RENTAL: anyone with children finds November 1 littered with leftovers of the night before. The size six costume Suzy wore last year wouldn't fit her this year, so you had to go to a size eight. These two sizes of one-night-a-year clothing, added to the size four already in the closet, plus the ones you purchased for Mary Lou which Suzy wouldn't be caught dead in (she doesn't even know who Wonder Woman was) – well, I think you get the idea. Your closet's limited space is filled with one-night stands. And you're not the only one in the neighborhood in that situation, so take advantage of it as a fundraiser for your favorite cause.

237 First of all, you have to let the neighbors and your relatives and other members of your group know you're collecting costumes (or old-fashioned clothing). The ideal time to do this is November 1 of any given year, but if you're reading this book in July, start now. Yes, your closet will probably reach capacity as the donations roll in, but it's for a good cause. Remember?

238 If a member of your organization has an extra closet in which the entire collection of costumes can be stored, take advantage of it. You might find it possible to store your costumes with those of the local ballet or theatrical group, with the understanding they can borrow your goodies for any productions that come along in the meantime, exclusive of Halloween. Be sure the costumes are in good shape – clean, pressed, and patched if necessary. Attach a card to each hanger or box telling which accessories go with each costume. Be sure the size is clearly shown to make "shopping" easier for your customers.

239 Hunt up your local media again, and make them aware of the availability of the costumes for local citizens. You don't want to say "children," because you will probably receive some outstanding adult-sized costumes, too. All the better. This just broadens your fundraising capabilities and gives your project a wider audience. You may get donations of old military uniforms, dance recital duds, hotel uniforms or even period clothing.

240 The period clothing has a distinct possibility of being an even greater treasure. There are "discovery" shops all over these days who will pay good prices for quality period clothing. If the old dresses or suits or hats (or shoes, gloves or whatever) are in wearable condition (without visible moth holes, tears, rotted fabric, etc.), don't expose them to being destroyed by a cavorting Halloweener. Locate a market for them and make money for your cause by selling them in their present good shape.

241 Some historical homes or museums, though without funds to purchase them, need this clothing for display, and will be happy to give receipts for charitable contributions to the donors. This is a service you might offer donors of such clothing if you cannot find a cash market for them. It is a goodwill gesture which will help insure that you receive all their donations of such items. It won't put money in your coffers, but it will certainly give your donors confidence in your organization's integrity.

242 Depending on the economy in your neighborhood, you can decide how to operate your HALLOWEEN COSTUME RENTAL business. You might just use a flat rental price or a deposit plus rental (for the very best costumes), or give a credit to anyone who donates a costume which in turn can be applied against the cost of his renting a different one. You might even go for a no-cash, two-for-one or three-for-one deal, wherein you rent one costume for a donation of either two or three costumes from the customer. There are any number of ways in which to handle it. The best one, especially since this book is about raising funds, is to require at least part of the rental to be paid in cash. Just before Halloween (maybe by September 15) put up your posters, advising folks when the "shop" will be open for business, and hang your fundraising hat on Halloween. A tall black witch hat, obviously.

243 HALLOWEEN COSTUME PARTY: another Halloween gimmick is to hold a costume party for either adults or kids, fitting your entertainment accordingly. You might line up some of the "creatures" from the haunted house to add to the entertainment. Call it a MONSTER BASH;

sell tickets in advance and decorate as for a harvest barn dance party, or even the Gay Nineties, Roarin' Twenties, Election Gala or Wild West. For teenagers, you could probably get by with just records or a local disc jockey (for which you will probably have to pay unless you convince him to do it for free for the charitable cause you represent). You might have an inside track to such – or other – entertainment. As always, use your resources.

244 For adults, advance ticket sales will go better if you promise a square dance trio (at least) or a legitimate band. There are relatively few public dances for adults anymore in most areas, and some of us just hunger for those good old days when we could do a bit of cuddling to the strains of some nice slow music. Take advantage of our nostalgia. It's all for a good cause. Have I said that before?

245 Line up some door prizes (either white elephants left over from your rummage sale, or donations from local merchants), and use tickets with stubs (see the chapter on Budget Barriers and make your own). You may just have found such a good idea that it will be requested as an annual affair. This means that you can build on what you've learned this year to make next year's bash even more fun and lucrative.

NEW YEAR'S EVE

246 The same idea – a dance – can be used for this holiday, with perhaps a dress-up theme as well. Combine it, if you like, and if it's legal in your area, with bingo (with donated gifts from merchants) and you'll have folks breaking down the doors to get inside. Sell advance tickets.

TWELFTH NIGHT

247 This is an old English day of celebration. It is really on the sixth of January and the obvious theme would be an Elizabethan one. Costumes could be jugglers (include one, if possible, for entertainment, even if it's only someone in your group who can toss three oranges and usually catch them), or dancers, serfs, lords and ladies of the manor or jesters. It's really amazing what a little imagination can do toward costumes for something like this. You don't have to dash to a rental agency for duds. A heavy bathrobe with added gold cords from draperies, and a high draped hat (similar to a witch's peaked hat) can make do for the classiest of ladies. Men can borrow a pair of dark leotards and a matching (or contrasting) long-sleeved knit shirt, and cover it with a tunic (made by cutting a head hole in the center of a long strip of material, belted at the waist). House slippers or ballet slippers or even those fuzzy little half-socks you can buy at the discount department store will do for shoes for the ladies, or the lords. Don't be scared of any costume situation. Almost always, there is an easy and inexpensive (not to say cheap) way to be among the best-dressed at any such gala.

248 Have entertainment. Tongue-in-cheek, even, like those jugglers we mentioned earlier. If your local school or church has a madrigal singers group, line it up, too. The refreshments are easy – hot spiced cider (you call it mead), cookies or shortbread, fruitcake, fruit of all sorts. Sell plenty of tickets in advance – enough to overfill your space, as some won't show.

LINCOLN'S AND WASHINGTON'S BIRTHDAYS

249 This is a natural time for a patriotic event. You can use either early American or typically American food, first of all. Of course, cherry pie is a natural for George's celebration. Costumes aplenty are still to be found due to our recent bicentennial celebrations, so that's another easy bill to fill. What you have to do is come up with an activity for your ticket purchasers. Will it be a homespun hoedown dance, ala Abe's day, or a more formal event honoring George? Of course, just taking orders for homemade cherry pies for February 22 might bring you a bit of change for your cause, if you have the pie-bakers willing to take on the chore.

250 You might take advantage of the talent in your local schools, invite the kids to present a short play or skit which carries out your patriotic theme, and have a potluck dinner for which the customers pay a dime a dip, or put on a bean and cornbread dinner, selling tickets in advance at a set price. Desserts can be made and donated by your members to cut down on expenses and add cash to your treasury. Send someone dressed as Abe or George to the local television station and get their attention – and some free publicity for your cause. Work with the local school or a particular teacher who'd like the opportunity to show off her class's talent, if your members can't handle that part of the event themselves. They probably are quite talented though, if you can only dig deep enough to find out what that talent is.

VALENTINE'S DAY

251 This is an absolute natural for a Sweetheart Dance. You might have a Mother and Son Dinner, or a Father and Daughter event. Have members of the opposite sex (of your members) serve the food and do all the work involved. This means advance ticket sales, and the better the entertainment you can dream up for the evening, the better your sales will be. Our local Sacred Heart Academy in Springfield, Illinois, has an annual Father and Daughter Dance which is always a success. They don't specifically use it as a fundraiser, but you might choose to.

252 You might just have a neighborhood Box Social, with the gals bringing boxes in which they have packed a meal for two (or change it around and have the men do the cooking for a change). The boxes are then auctioned off (find an auctioneer willing to contribute his talent to the cause) to the highest bidder, who then has the pleasure of the lady's company for dinner or perhaps even the rest of the evening.

253 The rest of the evening could include bingo, cards or even charades. The money paid for the meals goes into the club kitty and everyone gets a chance to socialize with someone different for a change. Make certain that the owner of each box remains a deep, dark secret until after the bidding is over; otherwise, the wallflower (every group has at least one) will be embarrassed by the low bidding on her box, which just might contain the best meal of all. You could also have a contest for the prettiest box (decorations) before the auction, with a prize to be awarded.

ST. PATRICK'S DAY

254 Ah, the luck of the Irish be with you! And it will, if you plan a fun celebration on this auspicious date. Why not a corned beef and cabbage dinner (dessert donated by members, if you like, to cut down on expenses), or even a green beer blast – if that's the way your neighborhood likes to go Irish and you are working with an organization whose principles are not anti-green beer. Have a parade, ending up at the meal place, which is fun, too. Sell tickets along the way (printed in green, of course) if your feast is not something that has to be carefully planned as to quantity ahead of time.

255 Sell advance tickets for a complete meal. Some recipes to be experimented with (well, no, they're not really *that* experimental – just different) for such meals are Irish Soda Bread, Scones and the like. They're easy, by the way. If you can't find a scone recipe (it's at the library), cheat and use your biscuit recipe (or that box of biscuit mix on the shelf), roll your ball of dough into a circle, and cut into triangles before baking. You can add currants or raisins, too, if you like.

256 Beer bread is an easy hot bread for such a meal. It's a batter bread and can be baked in the dining hall ovens, right on the spot:

3 cups self-rising flour
1 can beer
3 tablespoons sugar

Stir until mixed, right in the loaf pan. Bake about an hour at 350° F (test) and serve hot. It's OK cold, and like most breads, doesn't cut too well when just out of the oven, so give yourself a little time between oven and serving – five or ten minutes. It's really good served quite warm, and is a fun thing to make.

APRIL FOOLS' DAY

257 This is an excellent time to have a carnival or some other event where you provide the opportunity for your ticket purchasers to have just plain fun. One group we know organized several dozen "April No-Fools' Day Parties" across a state. Group members mailed an invitation which read, in part: "On the eve of a traditionally humorous date, at parties statewide, we will seriously dramatize our determination to REFUSE TO BE FOOLED BY __________ and to raise funds to carry out ______________________________." You can fill in the blanks to fit your needs. You might not wish to be fooled by disease or famine or ignorance or prejudice; and you could be determined to raise funds for a medical cause, a cause that needs funds for sustenance, or a cause that aids education. The possibilities are endless.

258 At the party or event itself, you can offer skits which help carry out your theme – perhaps making fun of a problem, but in the end giving a suggestion of how to solve it. Or you could opt for a carnival-type event with small booths lining your site, offering any number of inexpensive activities, such as a kissing booth, fish tank, dunk tank and, of course, refreshments. And perhaps some take-home goodies like pies and cakes, all guaranteed NOT to be jokes. If you want to give away a joke food, you might doctor some popcorn with white pepper, but go easy. You're just playing a joke, not trying to mortally wound someone's throat!

259 Be as corny as you like at an opportune time like this. Have a box in the corner covered carefully with a sign – a BIG sign – that offers the opportunity for customers to pay a nickle (keep it cheap – it soon adds up) to see the "baby rattlers." Inside the dangerous-looking box, under a grill and all sorts of other security measures (you might even keep it padlocked between times), the baby rattler turns out to be just that – a baby's rattle!

260 Again, use your resources – and keep your sideshow prices at a minimum. A nickle is best because parents won't object to spending five cents at a time, while they might balk at the same joke (or even one lots better) if they have to pay a quarter. Your outlay for someone with an elbow, hand and tongue won't bankrupt your treasury, and you can always find a box and a baby's rattle – without having to buy one.

MAY DAY

261 May 1 is a traditional day for celebration of spring. You might take advance orders for May Baskets (small handmade paper baskets filled with candy or with paper, plastic or real flowers, but don't go overboard buying real posies – there are lots of freebies growing on May 1) which your members will deliver on May Day. Your celebration can feature a May Pole, a dance – whatever sounds like fun. This is also Law Day by proclamation of the president, so you can tie in patriotism, too. This might be a great time to honor Leonard Lawyer who has been so helpful in answering your group's legal questions. Ask the mayor to issue a proclamation honoring Leonard; deliver a May Basket to him; serenade him; make him know how much you appreciate all he's done for you.

262 You can also sell candy – perhaps take orders for homemade mints which are delivered on May Day. Or take orders to deliver flowers or other gifts to shut-ins or persons in hospitals or nursing homes.

INDEPENDENCE DAY

263 What a day! What an occasion to celebrate! What a great way to raise funds for your group, and have fun and celebrate your country's birthday at the same time! Parades, picnics, band concerts, sack races, hot dogs, ice cream socials and barbecues. Wow!

264 If there's a parade, set up refreshment stands (you have to have really QUICK service!) along the way. Of course, for the folks who are watching, you can take your time, but the participants in the parade may just have time for a quick sip of something cool. Don't gear your sales to the marchers, obviously. Have a booth at the end of the parade route for them, with appropriate refreshments. Or at the staging area while they're waiting for the marshal's whistle to toot and set them marching.

265 If there is a traditional band concert in your neighborhood, set up the traditional ice cream social tables and chairs. Or it could be hotdogs served hot from the grill, with several grills in operation at the same time. The ice cream social will require some cake-baking by your members and their parents, and, of course, ordering and serving of the ice cream and a beverage. All that hotdog sales will require are the grills, food and someone to cook and serve. Same with beverages – you can make it as simple or as complicated as you like.

July is a hot month and watermelon is a great seller. You'll find some hints on selling this goody in the chapter on Booths.

266 If there's a ballgame going on, see if your group can profit by selling tickets, programs, popcorn, soft drinks, seat cushions, sun visors (hats), or by parking cars.

FRIDAY THE THIRTEENTH

267 This can be a fun way to raise funds. Lots of the ideas for Halloween activities can be modified to fit the occasion. You might sell tickets (at a price ending in 13 cents) to a thirteen-course meal (which your members prepare and serve), or have a carnival with fortunetellers, Chinese fortune cookies, ladders to walk under and black cats and broken mirrors (safe ones, of course) in every corner.

SADIE HAWKINS DAY

268 If you're a comic strip reader, you can't have missed "Li'l Abner" unless you were absolutely born only yesterday! Our calendars have their February 29 leap year every four years (this could also be a leap year event), but Al Capp's mythical village of Dogpatch had its annual Sadie Hawkins Day, when the gals got to chase the guys in an obstacle course, and Marryin' Sam, the preacher, was waiting at the end of the race to tie the knots for any bachelors who didn't get away from their feminine admirers. You don't have to be quite that desperate to get your members married off, but it's fun to give the gals a chance to invite the guys to something. And of course, they get to pay all the expenses for the evening.

269 They can also take their fellows gifts and corsages – a perfume bottle labeled "Eau d'Olympics" (tied with a big bow, of course) and a corsage made of vegetables, for instance. Or – you come up with crazy ideas for gifts and corsages. Just let your imagination run wild. (I'll bet you'll never come up with anything to surpass a legitimate corsage I once got, made of gardenias, which had already turned brown by the time they were delivered – but that's another story.)

CHRISTMAS

270 This traditional holiday is known for its craft sales, bake sales and caroling, and unless you have a really good thing going, you may just wish to pass it by and be one of the customers at someone else's fundraiser. You might like to have a HANUKKAH FOOD SALE, and in place of the Christian Christmas dishes, offer Jewish goodies. If you have no one in your organization who is Jewish and can guide you in the appropriate ways and dishes, ask the local rabbi to help, assuring him that your efforts will reflect truly on Jewish traditions.

271 Have an ICE SKATING PARTY. Work with your local ice rink and make a profit from your group's ticket sales. Or, if your area is in a location where ice skating is safe on a pond, hold the party there, selling tickets and perhaps even renting skates. Line up those skates which your members won't be using and borrow them for the evening, renting them to others for a nominal fee. But be sure you get a deposit if you're selling tickets and renting skates to the general public. You don't want anyone skating off with someone else's skates (as in anything else, you have to be realistic).

272 Have a SLEDDING PARTY, lining up sleds, selling tickets, and ending up somewhere where hot chocolate, coffee, cookies or donuts will be served.

273 Go CHRISTMAS CAROLING. Let one of your group wear a sandwich board which tells your audience the name of your group, and what you're raising funds for. And have a good-sized legend printed on the sandwich board which says, "All donations will be gratefully accepted." The board wearer should carry a large hat in which to collect funds. The sandwich board sign can easily be made with two pieces of poster board, to help it hang in front and back of its wearer.

FOUNDER'S DAY

274 This can be a date which applies only to the organization which you represent, or a date which applies to a happening in your community. Or someone you wish to honor. It's sort of a "make up your own holiday" thing, and you can also make up your own ways to celebrate it and to raise funds for your group, using a combination of the methods in this book or your own ideas.

HOLIDAYS TO STAY AWAY FROM

275 Usually, you should avoid Mother's Day, Father's Day, Thanksgiving Day, Christmas Day, Good Friday, Easter, Passover, Rosh Hashanah and Yom Kippur. These days fall on different dates each year, so check your calendars carefully.

Sometimes there are holidays, too, which do not lend themselves well to a celebration or a fundraiser for one reason or another. Perhaps this is because everyone travels away from home on those dates (unless you want to take advantage of those who travel to your vicinity), or because these holidays are too personal for families to want interruptions of the traditional celebrations. You know your community – you have to, if you're going to be a successful fundraiser for your organization. You will know which holidays I mean.

There are exceptions to every rule, of course, but we won't go into those right now. Perhaps never.

12 Sunday Every Day

Products from Herbs, Spices and Flowers; Printed Products; Recipes; Party Ideas; Races; Booklets; Banquets; Style Shows

Sunday Every Day

For those of you working with youth groups connected with your local church or synagogue, you already have a head start on many other organizations.

First of all, you have a location for your meetings, and usually the place to hold your fundraiser, unless you've selected something too large to hold in the sanctuary or dining room, or too rambunctious for a religious building, like a rodeo, perhaps.

The second advantage is that your group probably meets weekly year-round, and you have lots of time for planning, working, fundraising and spending your proceeds.

Add to that the fact that you are a group within a group; that is, you have a "captive audience" for your sales efforts – the other members of your congregation.

You also have that something special which belongs to a group which has for its example the ultimate Giver of Gifts, the provider of fishes and loaves for those less fortunate, and the epitome in demonstrating brotherly love. For "love" is truly a magic word when it comes to raising funds, although perhaps "blessed" is more appropriate than "magic."

It is love which provides adult leadership; it is love which inspires young people to work hard to raise funds for those less fortunate. Love has opened more doors, and softened more hearts – and raised more funds for the needy than all the earth's centuries of greed could ever accomplish.

Many of the projects in this book could be easily applied to church youth groups, but the Bible gives us many ideas for special projects which teach valuable lessons as they also aid in bringing in tithes for a religious cause.

276 There are many references in the Bible, for example, to the herbs which grew in biblical times. By combining those herbs with items on today's kitchen and grocery shelves, many unique gift items can be produced to be sold at bazaars, by special order or in whatever way your church's young people may choose.

An HERBAL HANDWASH, for instance, which will remove cooking and other odors, can be made by combining equal parts of dried thyme, sage and rosemary, and steeping in white vinegar. Packaged in a pretty bottle with a cork and colored ribbon, this might have a small tag attached, on which is printed an applicable Bible quotation.

I could make it easy for you by listing some of the many quotations about herbs, but it will be more fun if your young people find their own quotations. You can be sure they will also come up with some other useful information as they search through those wonderful pages.

277 The flowers of the Bible, too, can be useful for Sunday School groups raising funds. You can make your own DUSTING POWDER, for instance, by using plain old cornstarch, which you spray with cologne of a scent which will match some dried flower petals you've collected and pulverized. Use just a bit of the powdered flowers, and let the powder stand at least overnight in the sealed container you've decorated to help it sell faster. Small margarine containers, or other plastic or glass containers with lids, make suitable holders for the talc, and these, too, you can tag with a suitable Bible quotation, telling something about the flower and scent you have chosen.

278 Small HERBAL BATH POUCHES can be made (using Bible quotations as part of the decor) from small pieces of cheesecloth – about three inches square – which you fill with one tablespoon each of dried lavender, rosemary and thyme. The "recipe" for the bath should also be included:

> Fill tub with one inch HOT water. Steep pouch for five minutes and then remove pouch. Finish filling tub with water.

279 Another project which has to do with the herbs of the Bible is the compilation of a COOKBOOK with recipes using those herbs and spices – the more unusual, the better. Here again, your group has a head start on some of its peer groups, for chances are there is a handy photocopier or mimeographing machine lurking somewhere in the church building, already used for church bulletins, etc., and all ready to be put to use for your own small publication. This cookbook is then sold to the families and friends of your organization for profit.

Put your members to searching the Bible for suitable quotations which mention herbs and spices – or even foods themselves – and then use the quotation on the same page as the recipe which features a particular herb or spice. It's a lovely theme for a cookbook, and you can be as simple or as elaborate as you choose.

280 Lovely POTPOURRI or SACHET BAGS can be made using dried petals of flowers mentioned in the Bible. This is an easy project for even the least talented of fingers. Make the scent bags from odds and ends of ribbon and lace and pretty, porous fabrics, using simple square shapes for easy sewing. More talented youngsters may decide to go more ornamental, using fancier shapes for their sachet bags.

Really pretty SCENT BAGS can be made from remnants of lace if you remember to line the lace (which usually comes with holes in the pattern through which your potpourri could fall) with something like the good parts of discarded ladies' hosiery or pantyhose. Don't use too dark a shade unless you are also using a dark shade of outer fabric. The contents of your sachet bags can be a potpourri made of many different kinds of dried flowers, or spices like whole cinnamon or nutmeg, or a variety of scents.

281 Some of the nicest-smelling flowers for your sachets are roses, orange blossoms, violets, lily of the valley, lilac or honeysuckle. Herbs such as lavender, mints of all kinds and rosemary all lend much to a sachet bag. These can all be tagged with biblical quotations to carry out your theme. Thyme, basil, marjoram, coriander, dill, fennel and caraway are other herbs you might choose. If they don't have their roots in the Bible as well as your family herb garden, you can always find suitable legends and stories to put on your little tags by perusing the works of Shakespeare and books which deal with the background of such useful herbs.

282 You can carry out the flower or herb scents in other items for sale as well. Candles, pomanders (made by sticking whole cloves into apples or lemons), rose beads, rose jelly, rose butter and even crystallized rose petal candy can all be made from – or flavored and scented from – the flower that is usually found in every garden or lawn – the beautiful rose.

283 For some fascinating ideas and recipes – and even instructions on how to make beads out of rose petals –there's a charming little book entitled "Potpourri," by Ann Tucker Fettner, published by Workman Publishing Company of New York. In its pages, you are apt to find something to match many biblical mentions of herbs, spices and flowers. Make a trek to your local library and see what books there are about herbs, spices and flowers, and then tie in the information to your biblical theme. Then you can offer something to your customers that is not only useful, but is also a reminder of an ancient heritage.

284 Another project your church's youth group might like to take on is the printing of NOTE PAPER, PLACE CARDS and even POSTAL CARDS, using Bible motifs and themes. Using the herbs and spices idea once more, many delightful designs can be made on place cards or note paper. Use flower petals or herbs and spices which are glued with white glue onto the paper. Or some of your talented youngsters might draw, in pen and ink or watercolor, pictures of the biblical flowers or herbs.

285 Postal cards can be made with pretty biblical themes painted or drawn on one side, with the other side left for the address and postage. Check with the post office to make sure you purchase the right size of file card – 3" x 5" or larger. Package the cards ten to a set, tie with a pretty ribbon, and sell to your family and friends. The file cards are fairly inexpensive, and a little artwork can make them quite pretty. Postcards are useful little items for any household to have handy.

286 The cup or chalice is an object which has special meaning in religion. The sacrament of communion is common in many religions, and the cup can become an integral part of your organization's fundraising, as it can be used in many different ways.

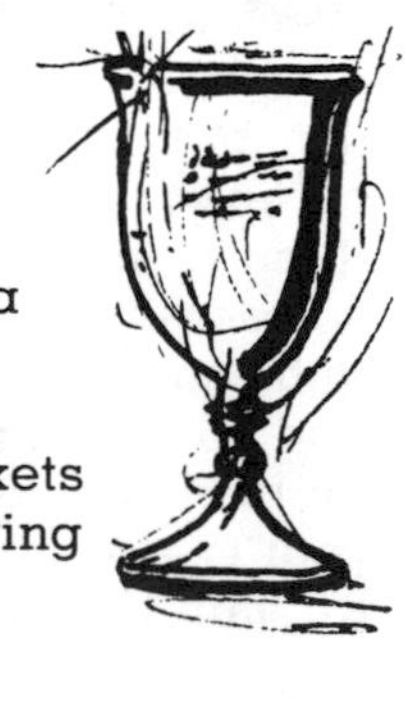

287 You might have a RECEPTION or TEA, to which you've sold tickets in advance. Or take a freewill offering during the event. The refreshments for the reception would, of course, include a beverage to be served in the symbolic cup, and would perhaps be a recipe which is itself significant. The refreshments and the use of the cup would be only a part of the event; your young people would provide some sort of program which would give all who attended something to enjoy.

288 The cup can also be used in fundraising, by SELLING A CUP itself. Take orders for a cup which would have a design significant to your cause – a design which would remind all those who use it of something special. You would need to decide on a cup design, take orders, and have a specialty company come up with the cups. Those companies are easy to find in the phone directory of any good-sized town.

Your fundraising cup might be a COFFEE CUP, a TEA CUP, a COCOA CUP, something to use daily, or it could be ornamental in design – something for the mantel or shelf at home – again, with its special, significant design.

289 There is mention of various woods in the Bible, also, which might give you ideas for fundraisers. Even the very gathering of firewood – to be sold in the neighborhood or congregation – is appropriate to your group. Wooden carvings, furniture – any number of things come to mind when we mention wood. Your kids can probably name a dozen ways they could tie in their biblical teachings with wood, and raise funds for their cause.

290 Many things occur in churches and synagogues which are meant to be remembered. Your group might take on a project to DECOUPAGE the many mementoes of special church events. The decoupaged items would then be sold to raise funds. Some of the things which might be decoupaged on pretty wooden plaques are wedding invitations, programs or announcements, baptismal certificates, memorial service programs and special musical programs. Any number of pieces of paper which would otherwise be thrown in a wastebasket can be preserved in a becoming manner by your young craft enthusiasts. But find someone who's skilled in the craft to teach you, and then grow from there.

291 Your young people might like to sponsor a CONGREGATION BIRTHDAY PARTY. To do this, select a host and/or hostess for each month of the year who is then responsible for preparing a table and providing a good-sized cake decorated suitably for each birth month. Guests go to the table of their own month to be greeted by the host/hostess, and then they share the communal cake. To take care of the overflow of any given month (when the cake isn't big enough for all who were born that month who attend), it is good to have a "church" cake, too, so extras can enjoy dessert from that cake. You can either sell tickets ahead of time (that's a good idea, to let you know how many to plan for) or have a freewill offering that evening. And, of course, your young folks have prepared a program for entertainment!

292 Another idea for raising funds for your church group might be to have a SUNDAY SUNDAE PARTY. You sell tickets ahead of time – to as many as you have room for – and then provide at least two flavors of ice cream, plates, plastic spoons and all sorts of toppings for the sundaes. If you can talk a local ice cream merchant into providing some of the goodies, that helps, too. Be sure to have both hot fudge and plain chocolate syrup, marshmallow creme, at least three kinds of nuts, whipped cream, candy crunchies and all sorts of fruit toppings (strawberry, pineapple, cherry and butterscotch and . . . I think you get the idea).

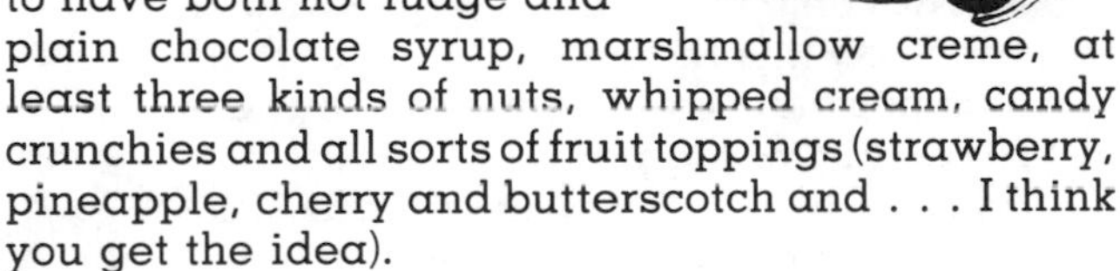

One note of caution: you'll have more luck selling advance tickets to men and boys, as gals tend to remember their diets more often; but you'll have to have more ice cream on hand for the gentlemen than you will for the ladies.

You can use the same idea with pizza. Provide the pizza shells and all sorts of toppings to be added before popping them in the oven.

293 When you sell tickets to a "FOOD PARTY," be sure to provide some sort of entertainment. If you are completely out of ideas for entertainment, you'd be surprised how much folks will enjoy an old-fashioned "sing-along." Be sure to provide song sheets to help remind the oldsters of the words, and to teach the words to the kids who have never been sentimental about music older than that sung in the last decade. If you have a piano player in your midst, like some one's grandparent, it really adds to the evening and closes more generation gaps.

294 Your kids might not be interested in sponsoring a marathon race, but some races can be really fun. How about holding a RACE NIGHT, when you sell inexpensive tickets to those present to participate in different events? One race might be a SHAVING RACE. Have two or more contestants competing to see: (1) how long it takes to paint another's face with shaving cream, and (2) how long it takes to shave it with a plastic spoon. You can think of all sorts of hilarious variations on this theme – and make them so ridiculous that everyone wants to buy a little ticket and participate. You might let the ladies in the group have a FACE RACE, where they compete in teams to see how long it takes to put on makeup and then remove it. Provide eyeliner pencil, eye shadow, blusher and lipstick – and cleansing cream and tissues.

295 Another race is a DRESSING RACE, where people buy tickets to compete by seeing how many articles of clothing they can get on in the shortest amount of time. Sell tickets for a RELAY RACE, where each contestant runs a specified distance to a dish of crackers, has to eat two crackers and then whistle a tune before running back to the finish line. Make the tickets cheap for the little kids, and more expensive for the older kids if you like, so everyone can participate – and every penny counts.

296 Another project which might just be a natural for a church group, especially if you have a nearby cemetery which has never been recorded, is to CANVASS THE PLOTS at the cemetery, recording the information from burial markers. Then have the information typed into book form, copied and sold to families and parishioners in the locality.

Such books, even if done halfway well (and I'm sure you'll want to do a super job) sell quickly because of the great interest in genealogy and historical research. The project can also turn into quite a treasure hunt which the kids will probably enjoy, if the stone markers are old and hard to read. This will require that they learn how to do rubbings, by taping plain paper over the inscriptions and then rubbing with chalk or crayon to bring out the legend so it is readable. This is not a project which can be done overnight, for it will take time to do all the copy work at the cemetery, get it typed into a neat book form, etc. But if you do a bit of advertising –not necessarily the kind you pay for – and let folks know the book will be available, you will have folks beating a path to your door to purchase your product.

297 Another project your group might like to do, and especially at Christmas time, is a GIFT-WRAPPING SERVICE. You could do it by appointment, with members going to subscribers' homes to wrap their gifts. Or subscribers could bring their unwrapped items to the church at a specific time to have them all wrapped and tagged. You need to decide ahead of time which method to use, and whether your group provides the wrapping material and charges more, or lets the subscriber provide the paper and ribbons, and your group charges less for the actual wrapping. If you provide the wrapping material, you can probably get a lot of donations from the closets of your members and friends, thus cutting down on your overhead.

298 There are many beautiful stories which your young church people have grown up hearing and which can give you valuable ideas for fundraising projects. For example, the story of Ruth and Boaz might lend itself to a HARVEST BANQUET, with reenactment of harvest procedures, as well as the ancient ceremonies connected with that important part of the year. Perhaps we already celebrate similarly at Thanksgiving, but there are many ways in which this ancient story could be told, in a PAGEANT – written by your members – with tickets sold ahead of time so you know how many to plan for.

299 The story of Joseph and his coat of many colors lends itself beautifully to a STYLE SHOW held in your church building, with clothing from your members' sewing machines, or a local clothier. You might even have a MEN'S STYLE SHOW, now that our men are more style-conscious and there is as much choice for them these days as there is for ladies.

Select your favorite Bible story and use it as a theme for your fundraiser. There are as many ideas in that beautiful Book-of-books as anyone could wish for.

300 And perhaps my favorite has to do with a ceremony closely associated with most religions – the breaking of bread. Your youth group might like to use this tradition in some way to raise funds for its project. One way is by having a BAKE SALE, with different varieties of bread being offered, and stressing the unusual or old-fashioned recipes. Bread is mentioned early on in the books of Genesis, Exodus and Jeremiah. The breads of the early centuries were very unlike the soft white bread we are accustomed to today.

Ancient breads were made of wheat, barley, rye and other grains, and were often unleavened (without yeast or other agent to cause the dough to rise). The loaves were made into various shapes and baked in earthen ovens, upon heated stones, or on hot coals, so you have a lot of leeway for your bread-baking.

Dig into some old recipe books and see how early American housewives made bread. Your library can probably provide you with recipes for bread very similar to that baked during biblical times, for the women of the Middle East are using the same methods and recipes today as were used at the time of Christ and before.

301 Just the baking of bread itself is a ceremony no child should miss out on. You are sure to have some adult in your vicinity who still knows this ancient art. Even before you start on your fundraising bread project, have this expert come to the church and get all your youngsters involved in their own bread-baking. Choose a simple recipe; have each child bring his or her own ingredients, or provide them all yourself; and get them involved. The story of the fishes and loaves will take on a special meaning as each child samples the loaf he has just created. After that, you're ready to start on the baking and selling part of the project.

There is something about the mixing and kneading of the dough and the waiting for the bread to swell to double its size which to me is spiritual. Even if your group never goes out into the neighborhood and sells a loaf of bread, its members will have learned something more precious than gold.

13 Just Ideas

Business Services; Contests; Recreational Events; Advertising and Promotional Gimmicks; Tag Days; Auctions; Calendars

Just Ideas

If your group needs to make $1,000, your members have a choice. They can either find one person willing to part with $1,000, or they can find 1,000 people who are willing to donate $1. I think we both know which is more realistic.

There are so many ideas for fundraising that this book could become an encyclopedia, but I'm sure I don't want to spend that much time writing, and you don't want to spend that much time reading. For that reason, this chapter will just throw the ideas at you, and let you take the ball and run with it, using some of the ideas that you've already read in this book for back-up.

301 If your neighborhood has a lot of swimming pools (lucky you), your group can become POOL-CLEANING TEAMS. Ditto for the cleaning of gutters and drain pipes. These jobs require ladders, the proper tools and adults to oversee both the job and the safety of the workers.

302 Spring is the traditional time for housecleaning, so you might provide the service of cleaning your neighbors' feather pillows and replacing the ticking. Consult with a granny or great-grandmother on this to make sure you know what you're doing. Feather pillows are very expensive to purchase these days, and you can't take the risk of losing someone's valuable feathers out the vent of the dryer, or of ruining someone's washer or dryer in the attempt. Seek advice on this almost-forgotten service. The new pillow ticking should be made ahead of time, of course, so it will be ready for the big day.

303 Your group might strike a bargain with the beauty shops or barber shops to share profits on a particular day, making certain that your members and their families and neighbors insure a full booking in every case.

304 If you have gardeners – particularly rose-lovers – you also have a need for rose bush fertilizer. Make a deal with the owners of the nearest riding stable to haul off their manure piles. You can charge $15 or more for a good-sized amount of manure and make everyone happy. Scooping it up and delivering it may not be the most aesthetic things your members have ever done, but you can be sure this activity will get lots of advertising. If there's no riding stable, look up the closest dairy farm.

305 How about CHARTERING A BUS TOUR of your area, with visits to historic sites or to businesses where you can see production going on? Some businesses to visit are: a dairy processor (warn everyone there's to be a certain aroma there), a bakery, a grain mill (especially those which have experimental kitchens or which manufacture cake mixes, etc.), a weaving factory, a greeting card manufacturer, or a large or small newspaper. Sell tickets ahead of time, making sure to fill the buses – that's plural because it's as easy to fill two as one if you just make up your mind to do so. Be sure that one of your stops will include refreshments. If the refreshments are at the bakery, all the better, because there's no charge. You might even have a winery in your vicinity, and I won't comment on any refreshments you might have there.

These tours should obviously be geared to either adults or children – or a combination of both – so that there is no possibility of children being taken somewhere unsuitable. Again, know your community, and plan accordingly.

306 If there are new homes being built in your community, why not make a deal with the contractor to CLEAN UP the finished house to make it ready for showing to prospective buyers? Fifty dollars per house should be the minimum fee, but be prepared to work – there'll be mud from dirty feet, fingerprints on the windows, sawdust, and various other types of dirt to dispose of. It won't be easy, but it's quite lucrative.

307 Sponsor a CAR RALLY. Talk to the motor vehicle division of your city, county or state government, and get official advice and help. Car dealers can give advice on this, as can car club members. A rally can be lots of fun for the participants and the sponsors. There are several ways to make money at this – entry fees, food stands, souvenirs, etc. – but there will also be a few expenses unless you find "angels," or backers, to purchase the trophies, pay the prize money, etc. Car dealers make excellent angels. Any time you find an angel for any of your projects, make sure you help keep his wings dusted and his halo shiny. We can't get along without them.

308 You might sponsor a BABY RACE. Babies who are unable to walk are placed on the outer edge of a large circle (or on a long race track), with a goody in plain sight at the center (or wherever the finish line is). The first baby to reach the prize is the winner. You can charge entrance fees or have betting on a half-and-half basis (if that's legal in your state), where the sponsor keeps half the bets placed on the racers. If you line up nice prizes from merchants, you keep all the entry fees. If you have several heats, and then a final, the money can add up quickly. A caution: babies don't stay awake or dry for very long periods of time, and their attention span is quite short, so don't drag it out too long. You'll have to set a reasonable time limit on each heat because if none of the racers reach the finishing line within a fair length of time, you could wipe out the entire time frame and not even have one winner. Have referees or judges to settle any altercations, and have some memento to give each baby (or parent) who takes part.

309 Another thing which attracts people and the media like crazy is another baby-oriented fund-raiser – a BABY CONTEST. Stay away, if at all possible, from titles such as "Prettiest Baby," because every parent knows his or her own baby is the prettiest in the whole world. And we wouldn't want all the non-winners (there are no losers in this type of contest) to live with a fractured ego the rest of their days.

You might choose titles such as "Healthiest Baby" or "Baby Looking Most Like (you choose the celebrity)," and stay away from the ego-shattering part of contesting. You should pick judges who know something about babies – at least some of them should, although a bachelor makes a great judge – like doctors, nurses, grandmothers (as long as their grandchildren aren't contestants), and perhaps the celebrity himself or herself (if he/she dares to get near this particular contest!). You should have a panel of judges – not just one – and give its members certain criteria for their judging. Again, line up prizes from merchants, and perhaps make the grand prize a contract for free pictures from a local photo studio for a given length of time. Charge an entrance fee, and sell tickets to those who want to watch the pageant, just as you would for the baby race. Obviously, you won't sell a ticket to the babies' parents – they've already paid an entrance fee. If the baby belongs to two sets of parents, its birth parents having divorced and remarried, the free tickets should be given to only its birth parents; the new steps have to pay to get in. After all, this is a fundraising project for a charitable group, and if you're too charitable, you'll wipe out all the profits.

Such "pageants" can be held for whatever age range you wish to be contestants. It's your baby – in more ways than one – you make the changes.

310 Another crowd- and media-pleaser is an old-fashioned FROG JUMPING CONTEST. Read Mark Twain for ideas for this one, and line up your prizes from local merchants who sell sporting goods – or from the fish market, perhaps. Sell tickets to those who watch, and charge entry fees to frog owners. Sell refreshments (but no buckshot, please) at each event you can, even if it's only popcorn or some other easy-to-make item.

311 Other old-fashioned events could include CONTESTS for stilt-walking, greased pole-climbing, greased pig-catching, sack races, wheelbarrow races, watermelon-eating, watermelon seed-spitting, pie-eating, walking on rails, hoop-rolling and many others. Talk to some grandparents for this one to get new ideas which are really old. And don't forget another Mark Twain goody – fence-painting.

312 Sponsor a RODEO or HORSE SHOW. If you have a local stable, work with its owners, or with the 4-H riding club, for the horse show. For the rodeo (a bit more audacious), talk to the people who run the arena or building where it would be held – they can line you up with the proper people and livestock.

313 Is there a navigable river or stream in your area? How about sponsoring a SCENIC BOAT TRIP, complete with entertainment from you, the boat crew or professional or amateur performers, all for the price of the ticket?

314 You can't have too much singing and dancing on board a plane, but many people would like the opportunity to take a short spin up in the clouds. Get together with the people at the airport and find out how you can sponsor SCENIC AIRPLANE RIDES. *Don't forget to talk to Leonard Lawyer about this type of activity.*

315 Hold a ROAST for a local celebrity or politician. Line up his friends to make appropriate remarks; sell tickets for the roast; and have it served at a local restaurant or hotel. This takes reservations, planning, etc., and you can't do it overnight, but a roast can be an excellent way to raise funds.

316 Have a FRUSTRATION AUTO SMASH. Find an old wrecked car. Remove the glass so no one can be injured if it breaks, and sell tickets for people to take so many swings at the car with a big rubber mallet. Work with your local car dealers and wrecking yards to make sure you know all the safety angles. Talk to our friend Leonard, too, as well as the local authorities. Your space will have to be roped off to keep observers from getting too close, and the advertising should state clearly that the liability is in the hands of the ticket-buying car-smasher. See what price works in your area. This event is popular with teen-age boys, naturally.

317 Sponsor a WAGON TRAIN for a weekend (or longer if you're *that* brave) camping trip. Hire wagons; have wagonmasters and expert campers to serve as trail bosses; figure up what the food and the rental of all equipment will cost, and add a good sum for profit for your group; and start selling reservations. The media will like this one, too. Only one thing wrong with this idea: it may be so popular you'll have to rebook for almost every weekend of the summer – but that's your problem, not mine. The profits you make will also be yours.

318 Work out a DISCOUNT TIE-IN with a local chain of grocery stores. Print up (meaning, copying machines to the rescue) sheets which are distributed throughout your area (try to saturate, not just distribute). Work this so that the grocer will pay your group a certain percentage of all sales on a particular day. Anyone who presents your sheet or brochure that day gets the discount. Then make sure every family in town heads for that particular store to do their weekly shopping. If the other stores' managers get upset, tell them they can each have a "day" of their own, as long as they give the same deal to your organization. Fair is fair.

319 If your group is craft-oriented, make up and sell a bunch of silk flowers, paper flowers, dried flower arrangements, bagels, macrame objects, origami, woven stuff, handspun yarns, hand-caned items, or even bonsai tree arrangements. If you have someone who is really gifted at any of the above, see if he won't serve as teacher at a SEMINAR on the craft which your group will sponsor, advertise and sell tickets to. You're using your resources again.

320 More publicity can be obtained by thinking up really hokey ways to get your project in the public eye. If you catch the media's eye (not just that famous network eye), reporters will run the play for you, almost all the way to a touchdown. That is something you have to do – make sure your idea makes contact on the right side of the goal line.

321 You can ask a local advertising firm for a FREE BILLBOARD in a conspicuous part (or parts) of town, and remind him that his donation is tax deductible. You can have BUMPER STICKERS made up to advertise the coming event and intrigue everyone into wanting to attend (and spend their money). You can sell bumper stickers to backers of your cause, making money and advertising at the same time.

322 T-SHIRTS are another great thing when it comes to fund-raising. Not only can they be made up and worn to advertise your organization and its goals or projects, but they can be sold as money-makers, too. I've known some kids to join an organization just because of the nifty T-shirts its members wore.

323 Once you get their attention, give them something fun to do. You don't have to stress to the kids all the time how worthy their cause is, as long as they're having fun while they're working. Then you'll have strength to add to your original nucleus of members and leader (which could mean your kids and you, which actually means just you. Don't let that happen.) Spice up your act. Make it fun. Make things happen. Do hokey things. Do funny things. Do even dumb things, as long as they're not dangerous, and do get attention. You don't have to act your age all the time while you are working as a youth leader – that's probably the real reason most of us do it. We can be "just kids" again. More fun!

324 Our Methodist church for many years sold a BIRTHDAY CALENDAR. Members and anyone in the community who wished to could have their names listed on the date they were born by paying a minimal amount (I think it was five cents), and the entire calendar was sold for something like a dollar. Ads across the bottom or top of the page were sold to local merchants, which also added to the income and profit. What a great surprise to wake up on your birthday and find the mail carrier laden with mail – all for you! Probably the greeting card industry should have subsidized the calendar, too, but we never bothered to look into that possibility. We definitely helped the postal department out of its red ink, though.

325 The Muscular Dystrophy Foundation makes it easy to hold a fundraiser for the benefit of its charity. Its members have kits all made up and ready for distribution at your request if you wish to hold an event to raise money for them. If you've never worked for this particular group, you might want to have your own organization support such a benefit. You'll not only do a very good deed, you'll also get some excellent ideas for your own fundraising activities. MD needs your support – and so do many other such groups – so work with them and for them, and benefit everyone involved.

326 Have a TAG or BUTTON DAY, where you sell buttons or tags supporting your cause, just as the veterans' groups have their poppy sales. The Badge-A-Minit people can help you make up your own badges quickly, easily and inexpensively, for sale on that day. And it's even fun making all those badges. I promise.

327 Fresh Christmas greens are available, but you might also want to SELL CHRISTMAS TREES. Line up your source in plenty of time. This event may even have to wait until the second Christmas after you decide to hold it, because trees are ordered from season to season, and next year's are probably already booked for sale by other organizations or dealers. Contact your state forester or the Department of Agriculture for the names of tree growers, and for information on what you'll need to know for this project.

328 Sponsor a USED CAR AUCTION in conjunction with a local car dealer. He usually sells most of his oldest-model trade-ins at auction anyway to commercial buyers, so see if he'll let you in on the act. Ask him to let you have a percentage of the sales if you do the publicity, and maybe even sell tickets and sell refreshments the day of the sale. If one dealer doesn't like the idea, go to a second, or a third, or . . . You know what I mean. Perserverance pays off with money for your treasury.

329 Have a local author who's interested in your organization? See if he'll give you a percentage of the profit from the sales of his next book if you, again, do all the public relations work for him, like lining up places and dates for autographing sessions, getting media coverage, etc. Make sure the book he's selling isn't one which would reflect badly on your youth group (although that type of book gets plenty of PR from the publisher and you wouldn't have a chance to get in on the act anyway).

330 If you haven't already decided to do something different, how about a FASHION SHOW ON SKATES? Obviously, you have to have rather specially-skilled models, but if your town has a skating team or derby-type operation, it could make you quite a bit of money. Work out the regular angles with clothing merchants (including any damage to clothing in case of an accident – if you use professional or semi-pro skater/models, this should be no problem), door prize donors, publicity, ticket sales, etc., and put the money on ice. It really isn't a rinky-dink idea – just a bit crazy. And you have to admit, it's different!

331 If you aren't tired by now, I am. The big event is all over, the mess is picked up, the profits have been taken to the bank. Now what?

First of all, have a committee meeting and MAKE A LIST of everything that went wrong. You need that information for next year, as much as you need the list of "things to do."

Next, even though I'm sure you've properly thanked all the merchants who donated prizes or services, and all the public officials who gave you a boost, and all the media people who got people's attention for you, you've probably forgotten the most important people of all. THANK YOUR MEMBERS – and those in their families – who worked so hard. Thank them, thank them, thank them. If you've surpassed your fundraising goal and can possibly do it, give them some sort of reward. It doesn't have to be fancy.

One of the most prized trophies awarded at the annual state conference of the Illinois Children of the American Revolution is called the Mansion Ghost Award. It's really an absolutely horrid caricature of a weight lifter. It got its start when someone put a quarter into a slot machine at the Illinois State Fair, and molten plastic, in a horrendous magenta-purple color, poured into a mold and shortly cooled. The machine ejected the little man into the hands of the waiting fair-goer. Somewhere along the line, our little man was put into a rummage sale held by the Daughters of the American Revolution chapter which had purchased and restored an historic home of one of Illinois' former governors, and to no one's real surprise, was not sold. It ended up in a store room at the governor's mansion, and when the C.A.R. helped do some fall cleaning, was found in all its horrible splendor.

Too horrible to throw away, it was spray-painted a gold color (cheap paint – it ran in streaks) and given as a prank trophy at that year's state banquet. In later years it was placed on a lovely walnut base, and each year is gleefully awarded to a lucky recipient who treasures it until he passes it on the next year.

See what I mean about prizes? And kids? The kids are so wonderful they'd often really like something terribly hokey as a prize instead of all the plaudits which could be handed them in public, which would probably only embarrass them into not showing up at any more events. Of course, nice gifts like T-shirts are seldom turned down.

The greatest thing about working with kids is that they are so natural. Don't try to fake it with kids; they know every time. If you level with them, they'll return the favor. And then they'll work like slaves on your next fundraising project.

An example of letting your young members make their own choices might be seen in the next two examples of fundraisers.

332 My son's local Future Farmers of America chapter takes orders for citrus fruits every fall, with delivery just before Christmas.

We all benefitted – the chapter and those of us who ate that lovely, healthy fruit. If your group members want to do something like this, talk to a local wholesale fruit dealer. He will give you his best information because he probably has kids who are trying to raise money for their clubs, too, and because he is sure your club sales won't cut appreciably into his wholesale market. He might even do the ordering for you himself, as the Springfield, Illinois, wholesale dealer did for us when we needed watermelon in early July.

333 I couldn't get this near to the end of my book unless I suggested a spaghetti dinner – but a spaghetti dinner with a difference – a MILE OF SPAGHETTI DINNER. How do you determine how much is a mile of spaghetti? Measure a piece of spaghetti, divide into the number of inches in a mile, and go from there. Weigh it, and cook, serve and price it accordingly. The spaghetti won't taste any different, but the atmosphere in the dining room will be quite different. If your guests aren't eating their meal and all its trimmings, they'll be laughing, enjoying the audacity of eating a mile of spaghetti.

At your after-the-project meeting, discuss with your members their feelings about the event. Did they enjoy it enough to want to do it again? Or did they find too much of it boring? Boring is a major kill-word for fundraising. That's why hokey is so good. It's a long way from boring. It's fun. Many groups would find taking orders for grape-fruit (or wreaths, candy or popcorn) boring, and not want to do it. They want action.

Other groups would prefer this type of project, especially if they are involved in lots of other activities. Again, you have to know your resources, including your members' capabilities and proclivities, and decide which route your group should take next year.

The perfect fundraising project exists, I believe, when you've been able to make it so exciting and so much fun that you could begin selling tickets for next year's repeat event the day after this year's event ends. If you find something like that, hang onto it. If it is really a super-fantastic project, you might even see about having the idea and the methods copyrighted. Leonard, what would we ever do without you?

14 Party-party or Door-to-door

Party Sales; Commercial Fundraising Products; Legitimate Commercial Firms That Will Help You

Party-party or Door-to-door

Although I have tried to stress the more individualized type of fundraising for your organization, a book of this type would be remiss if it did not list the ways you can utilize the ideas of commercial firms, as well as their products, in raising money to help your cause.

334 Many groups have had success sponsoring parties, either in their homes or in church basements or school gymnasiums, where a representative of a national firm brings in merchandise, displays or demonstrates it, and gives the organization a percentage of the total sales made at the party.

The names and addresses of such party firms, which have maintained high visibility and high-quality merchandise, are listed below:

TUPPERWARE (plastic housewares, toys, planters)
Orlando, Florida 32802
(305) 851-4600

SARAH COVENTRY (costume jewelry)
Newark, New York 14593
(716) 454-7330

SHAKLEE CORPORATION (nutritional supplements and foods, personal care and household products)
1990 Powell Street
Emeryville, California 94608

HOME INTERIORS AND GIFTS
(decorative home accessories)
4550 Spring Valley Road
Dallas, Texas 75240
(214) 386-1000

STANLEY HOME PRODUCTS (household products, personal grooming aids, brushes)
333 Western Avenue
Westfield, Massachusetts 01085
(413) 562-3631

BEELINE FASHIONS (clothing)
100 Beeline Drive
Bensenville, Illinois 60106
(312) 860-3200

MARY KAY COSMETICS (makeup and skin care products)
8787 Stemmons Freeway
Dallas, Texas 75247
(214) 630-8787

PRINCESS HOUSE (decorative home accessories)
455 Somerset Drive
North Dighton, Massachusetts 02764
(617) 823-0711

AVON PRODUCTS, INC. (cosmetics, jewelry, personal care and some home products)
New York, New York 10019
(212) 546-6015

WATKINS PRODUCTS, INC. (seasonings, flavorings, spices, some cosmetics and home products)
Winona, Minnesota 55987
(507) 457-3300

Some of these companies have party plans which are conducted on a company basis, and some have to be established with the individual salesperson. Many of these companies are advertised in your phone directory's yellow pages so you can locate a dealer easily.

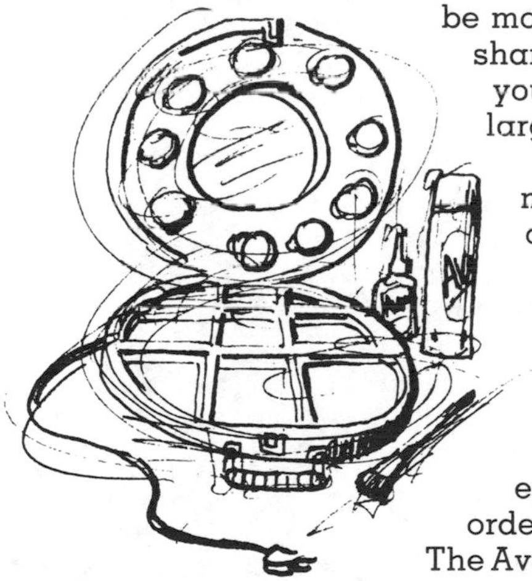

335 Don't wait for the Avon lady's "ding-dong" at your doorbell; look her up in the phone book and tell her your group is interested in HOLDING A PARTY. She makes 40 percent on most of the items she sells, and probably will be more than willing to share that with you if you guarantee her a large room filled with potential customers. She sends an order to her distributor every two weeks. Deliveries are shipped to her within a week, so you can expect timely delivery of all the items ordered at your party. The Avon firm offers a 100 percent guarantee on every item they sell – an outstanding offer. Avon dealers also work toward various prizes which are offered only to those dealers whose sales are the highest in the district or area. This is another reason a local dealer probably will be willing to work with your group – it could mean a trip to Hawaii or Europe or some other fabulous prize for her – and your group can help her win! (There are also quite a few male Avon "ladies," though.)

336 Many of the firms listed above operate similarly to Avon, so if you want to go this route, do so. You should provide light refreshments for your guests, but that, and the postage stamps for your invitations, or the time taken to call your guests, is all you will have invested.

337 The DOOR-TO-DOOR SYSTEM OF SELLING someone else's stuff can also bring in quite a bit of loot for you. It is fairly simple to decide what you want to sell, from whom to order it, how much you need to sell to meet your goal, and then to set aside time for your members to canvass the neighborhood with candy, popcorn or what-have-you in their trusty little hands.

338 For these items, as any Girl Scout leader can tell you, you have to have STORAGE ROOM to keep the cartons of merchandise until it's all sold. And by storage, I mean safe, clean and free from rodents, flood waters, heat or thieves. Your merchandise should also be free from pets, who can turn into particularly nasty little thieves or vandals. This usually means garages or

basements, and you know your garage and basement the best; would you take the minister's wife into yours? If not, you'd probably better look for another storage place, or another item to sell. The merchandise has to be clean – to the point of being pristine – if you're going to be able to sell it, because most of it will be used for personal consumption or gifts. That's what your public expects –quality in all regards.

339 Some of the firms with which I have dealt, or about which I have had good recommendations from friends, are listed below. When you order from such firms, find out if you can return unsold merchandise if it's undamaged. You can't sell chocolates in Christmas wrapping at Easter time, even if they would still be in very good shape by then. As mentioned before, don't try to send out boys to sell feminine stuff; they won't and it won't.

340 Some of these firms charge you less for what you purchase from them if you order more items. Some use a flat rate. If your group consists of only ten little blue-uniformed Camper Girls, your group would probably have a difficult time selling 2,000 or 3,000 pounds of candy or popcorn or that many bottles of vanilla, unless the girls all have parents and grandparents who work offices where such sales are permitted. If you do have access to such offices, keep track of them, and make sure you have members/parents canvassing them for sales. And likewise, if there are businesses which routinely post a sign prohibiting soliciting, don't send your little Camper Girls in with their satchels of sales items; it'll be embarrassing for everyone concerned, and may send your girls running to join some other organization.

The order of listing does not denote any special recommendation of one firm over another. These firms are listed in the order they appear in my original notes:

KATHRYN BEICH FUNDRAISING CANDY
1001 Roosevelt Road
Westchester, Forest Park, Illinois 60153
(312) 343-5828

OLD-FASHIONED CANDIES
6210 Cermak Road
Berwyn, Illinois 60402
(312) 788-6669

MISS DOLLY MADISON
BUTTERNUT BREAD, INTERSTATE PRODUCTS
8020 Kennedy Avenue
Highland, Indiana 46322
(219) 972-0180

ACE PECAN COMPANY
2055 Lunt Avenue
Elk Grove Village, Illinois 60007
(312) 364-3275

SHERWOOD FOREST FARMS
(fresh Christmas greenery, wreaths, etc.)
P.O. Box 789
Chehallis, Washington 98532
(206) 748-8367

MARION KAY
(seasonings, spices, vanilla extract, etc.)
ORIGINAL HOUSE OF FLAVORS
Brownstown, Indiana 47220
(812) 358-3000

WATKINS, INC.
(vanilla extract, spices, etc.)
Winona Minnesota 55987
(507) 457-3300

NOBLE POPCORN FARMS
Rural Route #3
Sac City, Iowa 50583
(712) 662-4728

BADGE-A-MINIT
(professional-looking badges you make at home)
Box 618, Civic Industrial Park
LaSalle, Illinois 61301
(815) 224-2090

HIGH CREST GREETINGS, INC.
(cards, gifts of all sorts)
6218 North Second
P.O. Box 2276
Rockford, Illinois 61131
(815) 633-4044

CURRENT, INC.
(stationery, cards, gifts, crafts)
Current Building
Colorado Springs, CO 80941
(303) 593-5990

Ada Castellani
(leather gloves, silk scarves)
Via Principe Ameda, 2-C
00185, Rome, Italy
(They do not offer a fundraising program, but you can use their products to set up your own.)

THAMES PECANS
(excellent pecans, walnuts)
P.O. Box 2206
Mobile, Alabama 36652
(205) 433-1689

AMERICA'S BEST
(Reeses, Hershey, M&M candies, etc.)
P.O. Box 121
Mobile, Alabama 36601
(1-800) 633-6750

I'm sure there are many more excellent firms with outstanding programs to help you raise funds, but these are the ones with which I am most familiar and, therefore, see fit to recommend.

341 Just a couple of notes: Current has a really classy line of materials, but although they've recently improved their delivery time, they still take a considerable length of time to deliver, considering few, if any, of their products are personalized. When you write them, tell them to send you the catalogs which show only the retail prices; otherwise, they bombard you with lovely catalogs which you can't show to your customers because they show the retail and two wholesale prices (which depend upon the volume you order). Current usually includes samples with their catalogs, which is a nice touch.

342 High Crest, on the other hand, handles good-quality goods. Although not all they handle is in the Cadillac or Continental category, *they ship the day the order is received*. You can also place orders by phone with High Crest, and all their staff seem most helpful.

343 Ada Castellani, a European firm, handles high-quality merchandise at excellent prices, ships in good time, and will also take small orders. You can mark your price up to make your profit; their prices are about half what you will pay in a local store.

344 Badge-A-Minit is another firm which ships very quickly, and has an excellent line of equipment at low prices. They also have ideas for how your group can quickly make personalized pins or badges to sell at a profit or just to advertise your particular cause. They will also make personalized sew-on labels for your group if you need them for uniforms, booster clubs, etc. All their prices seem quite reasonable, whether for promoting your group, or for getting plans for items to make and sell yourselves.

345 Another firm, which is not listed above, but is one from which I have

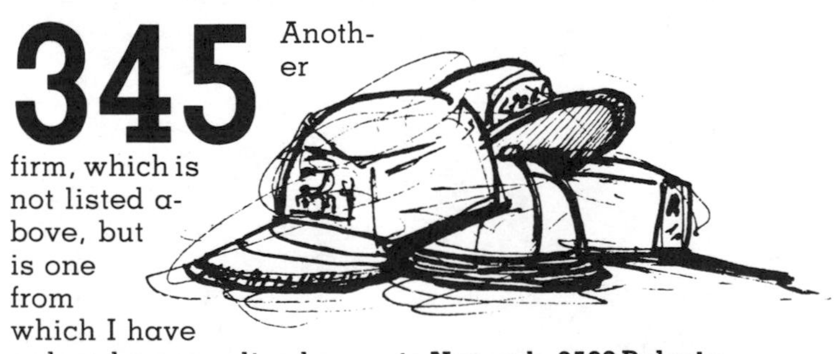

ordered personalized caps, is **Namark, 3580 Polaris, Las Vegas, Nevada 89103, (1-800) 634-6271**. They have adjustable caps (baseball caps or farmer-style caps) and will duplicate your design or logo on their caps at no extra charge. The initial charges for the caps are reasonable, too, and vary according to volume.

346 The Girl Scouts and several other youth organizations also sell items, such as cookies, which are specifically designed for their group. The Illinois Grand Assembly, Order of Rainbow for Girls, packages a box of candy (several flavors) which is specifically used for that group, and I am sure there are others.

347 The firms listed in this chapter are just a drop in the bucket. You probably have any number of reputable companies in your own community who have programs for fundraising, or who are willing to help you come up with something original while selling their product lines. Look over your community – you may be missing many good opportunities for fundraisers for your organization. If you can't find anyone, pick from my list, or go to your local library. If all else fails, contact the **American Association of Fundraising Council, Inc., 500 Fifth Avenue, New York, New York 10063**, and ask for the council's list of publications.

15 Things I Almost Forgot

Guidelines; Children, the Greatest Resource; Happy Laughter Mends Fences and Builds Bridges

Things I Almost Forgot

There is no way that any one book on fundraising could include all the possibilities, and I make no claim to having done so in this book. I do hope that the ideas here are, at least in part, different from those you've already heard about or perhaps tried for your own youth organization.

347 I could have talked about book-lending libraries, using books donated by members and collected from neighbors, but that has been handled in other books. I might have mentioned more ways of holding style shows, but I believe that if you go with the basic idea, you can bend it to suit your own needs and your own ideas. It's been a popular fundraiser for years, so I could add little to expertise already available to you.

348 I might have included patterns for craft items for your boutiques and bazaars, but the magazines on the shelves of your local book store or grocery store have new and exciting ideas galore.

I suppose I might have told you about all the hard work you're going to be doing as a youth leader, but if you didn't have that figured out before you took the position, it's too late now.

I do have to say that while it may be hard work – and take hours and hours of time which might be spent cleaning your own house, or reading, taking courses at your local college, or even – heaven forbid – writing a book yourself – the hours you spend with those kids will be something you'll never forget. The returns on your investment will be never-ending. We still open the door and see standing just outside boys and girls – hungry grins shining – who were contemporaries of our oldest daughter, married now quite a few years and living miles away. Those same kids are grown up now themselves, and many are involved in youth work in their own communities, but they have not forgotten the way – even though it's off the beaten track by quite a few miles – to our house. We'll probably be grandparents by proxy long before our own children decide to start their own families. It's a feeling you can't buy with money.

Of course, the owners of those hungry grins know their way to the refrigerator, to the pasture to visit the buffalo, to the back porch where the kittens hide out, and to where the sleeping bags are kept, in case they forgot their own. Youth leaders are special people. I feel very special, having spent my time with kids. Their eyes are wide open. They know a phony when they see one. They are waiting for new ideas, and they have plenty of their own. They live up, or down, to our expectations of them, and if we have high expectations, they'll go all the way to the top. They have faith; where's ours?

I suppose what I'm trying to say is, the next time you answer the phone and it's your priest or minister, or the lady at the Home Extension office, or the school principal, and he or she needs someone to lead the youth group, don't say no. How can you say no to an insurance policy which keeps you perpetually youthful, perpetually moving, perpetually excited and doing things? Shame on you if you even consider saying no.

Most youth organizations have excellent guidelines which come down to you through the levels of administration from the national office. Make yourself familiar with them. Take time to read and understand them – don't just stick them in the drawer and forget them.

I believe that of all the organizations we've worked with, the National Society Children of the American Revolution has the best-planned format for its youth. Annually, the national officers and chairmen plan, in detail, the goals of their program and steps to meet those goals. After these are approved by senior leaders, the young people spend most of their summer attending regional meetings, where the program is given in written form, and is followed by verbal explanations, discussions and questions from the floor. There is also almost always a delightful skit which more concisely depicts what's what on a particular project. You go away from their regional meetings so enthused and hyped, you can hardly wait to get home and start to work! I would never have believed it if I hadn't attended many of their meetings. If more organizations would get their acts together in similar ways, there would be thousands more boys and girls involved in active youth organizations, instead of lounging on street corners, indulging in activities we don't even want to think about.

Some organizations are oriented to the individual, as is 4-H. The goal of each member is to prepare an excellent project and win a blue ribbon, and ultimately the purple grand champion rosette. Other organizations, such as the C.A.R., are more group-oriented, with all projects being carried on as a society (the name for each local organization).

Either way is fine for some children, but not all. Some young people need the added incentive of owning that blue ribbon and taking it home with them. Others feel more comfortable working within the group concept in reaching goals.

You, as a parent, need to know which group might be best for your children. You may even have one child who needs to be individually oriented, and another who needs the group route.

You, as a youth leader, need to know which type of group you are responsible for, and how best to fit the odds-out child into the overall program. There is a niche in both types of organizations for that odds-out child, but it sometimes takes a while to figure out just where it is. If you have a member who is gung-ho when it comes to blue ribbons, but blasé about doing things the whole group will get credit for, you need to channel him or her into the part of the required work which gets the biggest spotlight. This will probably be the child who will make the best presiding officer or committee chairman, but will be lousy at cooking hotdogs or selling candy door-to-door.

The child who needs to find comfort with other kids of his own age and interests probably will excel at sales, but will be totally unable to make a speech before a meeting, let alone have to speak before adults. He'll probably make great posters.

Children are, therefore, the resource I am talking about. Know your resources, I've preached over and over again. Know the kids in your group; know what makes them tick, what scares them to death, what they like, how they listen, how they talk, and even how they laugh. Make sure there's lots of laughing. Happy laughter mends fences and builds bridges faster than any carpenter or engineer ever born.

I'm sure there are lots more things I've forgotten, but I can't think . . .

The egg?

I promised you an egg story? Are you sure I wasn't just playing a yolk on you? (Sorry about that – I couldn't resist!)

Okay, if you insist. Next chapter, please.

16 Eggzactly What You Need

Eggs-agerating the Value of Neighborhood Eggs; a Great Fundraising Idea

Eggzactly What You Need

An egg? I've been promising to tell you how to raise funds for your group using an egg? How dull!

349 Let's see if I remember how you do it. Oh, yeah . . . First, you buy 500 baby chickens and put them in cages in the living room . . . Nope, that's the wrong egg story.

The right egg story goes like this:

At a specific time on a designated day, all the members of your youth group are ready to begin canvassing their neighborhoods for an EGG SALE. Does each mother have to rush out and buy several dozen eggs? Do the eggs have to be hard-boiled, colored, blown, or what? What do the kids *do*?

What each kid does is to go to the house next door and explain to the lady or gent of the house that the Scouts (or 4-H members or whatever) are raising money for camp or uniforms (or whatever). All the club member asks of the first neighbor is *one egg*. That's right. Just one egg! Who wouldn't donate one dinky little egg (OK, so the sign at the store said, "Grade AAA Large") to this darling, big-eyed child who's obviously doing something for a good cause? So, a trip is made to the kitchen, one egg is retrieved from that long, narrow box in the refrigerator, and is handed to said big-eyed child.

The child says a big, big thank-you, and goes on to Neighbor Number Two.

Neighbor Number Two answers the doorbell, and is greeted by those same big, beautiful eyes, and two well-washed hands carefully holding *one egg*. The small club member (although there's obviously no age limit to this gimmick) explains that the Scouts, etc., are raising money for camp, etc., and asks Neighbor Number Two (NNT) to buy the egg. "How much?" asks NNT. "Whatever you want to pay," answers CMWBE (Club Member With Big Eyes). So NNT goes to the desk, pulls out money (often a dollar!) and hands it to CMWBE, who dutifully hands over the egg.

Now CMWBE goes to Neighbor Number Three, asking for the donation of one egg. It is then "sold" to Neighbor Number Four. I think you get the picture.

Of course, the handling of things as fragile as eggs can result in laughter, extreme care and even panic. The club members can carry a small Easter-type basket for their precious egg's transportation, or a tissue-padded box, or just trust the egg to the care of their own hands and their skill in climbing porch steps without tripping and destroying their "product."

You obviously wouldn't send little kids out to do this trick in a business district – not too many eggs there of the type you'd want – and no housewives who want to carry an egg around for the rest of the day. Neither would you trust your precious kids to a neighborhood where safety was a factor. Again, this should be done in your own neighborhoods, where you are already, I hope, familiar with its residents, its streets and its resources.

The kids may have to answer questions concerning the condition of the egg – whether it's rotten, boiled, or what, and the obvious answer is that it came fresh from the refrigerator of the next-door neighbor.

It's a fun idea for which no up-front funds are required; in fact, it needs no investment at all, as I won't talk about the time I spend working for various organizations. If this time were fully tax-deductible – valued at even minimum wages – it would drastically cut into taxes upon which our local, state and federal governments depend.

All I can say about this project is that it is better than scrubbing floors (although we've raised money that way, too), and more fun than watering the neighbor's flowers. I suppose it would constitute a major disaster if some lovely homemaker gave a child a dozen eggs. For heaven's sake, don't let that happen, as it takes away all the fun.

Don't worry about which came first, the chicken or the egg. Just keep in mind that what comes after the egg is more cash for your organization's treasury, and that's what this book is all about!

17 Diagrams For Booths, Etc.

Construction Designs; Materials Needed; Decoration Ideas

Diagrams For Booths, Etc.

Included on the next pages are simple diagrams which show the materials required for building a U-SHAPED BOOTH from which your organization's foods or other products can be sold and served. It can easily be built by amateur carpenters, mothers and even four-thumbed fathers. Storage space between uses is also taken into consideration. The booth can be stored almost completely flat between uses, and then put together again fairly quickly. The overhead sign can stand proudly in one end of your garage when not in use.

The instructions for the overhead sign are courtesy of T. Henry Abel, a young man from Illiopolis, Illinois, who is an honorary state president of Illinois C.A.R., and past national officer and chairman of the organization. He knows all about raising funds for C.A.R., Future Farmers of America and 4-H, and how much fun that can be. The overhead sign can be stationed over a card table(s) or used as a background for an open exhibit or sales booth.

It obviously is not required that you go to the expense and work to build a booth for your group's fundraising projects, but if you anticipate future projects (and what organization doesn't), a permanent booth can come in handy. The booth and/or overhead sign also adds to the overall picture you present to your customers, and makes sales easier by providing a compact and sturdy place from which to conduct business.

Three tables (which you will now learn how to construct) will be needed to complete your U-shaped booth. The tables are made from ⅝"-thick plywood (which comes in 8' x 4' size), cut into pieces two feet wide and eight feet long.

Before giving you the list of materials you will need to obtain before beginning to build your booth, I would like to mention your legs. Not *your* legs, actually, but those of the tables which will make up your booth.

You can purchase sturdy metal fold-down legs at your local hardware store. They may cost more than making your own, but they make your table construction much easier if you're short on carpentry talent. If you decide to purchase metal legs, then you should skip over the section which follows, which pertains to building the table legs. The metal folding legs will come with instructions and probably the right hardware for attaching the legs to your tabletops.

MATERIALS NEEDED FOR TABLES:

Lumber:	3	2' x 8' x ⅝" plywood (1½ sheets of plywood for tabletops)
	6	1" x 4" x 22½" (ends)
	6	1" x 4" x 8' (sides)
Nails:	6d (six-penny) size	

Two 1" x 4" x 8' and two 1" x 4" x 22½" pieces of lumber are nailed on the outside edge, under the plywood top, to make a skirt effect, so you will have a shallow box when you're finished. See **FIGURE 1**. Use coated (or ring-shanked) 6d nails about every eight or 10 inches.

MATERIALS NEEDED FOR LEGS AND BRACES:

(Skip this part if you purchase metal table legs.)

Lumber:	4	2" x 2" x 32" (legs)
	2	1" x 4" x 22½" (for hinge plate)
	4	1" x 2" x 24" (for "X" brace)
	4	1" x 2" x 30" (for leg brace)
Nails:	16	1¼" wood screws (to attach hinge plates)
	8	1¼" wood screws (for leg braces)
	4	T-hinges with screws

The above material will make legs and braces for one table. Your booth utilizes three tables, so multiply the above materials by three.

To make the legs for your table, use a 1" x 4" x 22½" piece of lumber, flat side down, as a hinge plate for attaching the legs. Attach the legs two feet from each end of the table, using 1¼" flat-head wood screws on the hinge plate. Neophytes, please note that there are all sorts of screws, so be sure to use *wood* screws, not metal screws.

Insert the screws from the top. Each leg is made using 2" x 2" x 32" lengths of lumber for legs. The legs are braced by forming an "X" brace with 1" x 2" x 24" pieces of lumber, with the legs spaced 18 inches apart, as show in **FIGURE 2**. When you attach the brace between the legs, alternate the "X" brace pieces so one is in front, and one in back, where they are joined to the leg lumber.

Attach the legs to the 1" x 4" hinge plate with T-hinges. Be sure to attach hinges on the inside, so legs will fold toward each other under the table when not in use. See **FIGURE 3**. The hinge plate is a reinforcing strip of wood attached between the tabletop and the legs.

Use a 1" x 2" x 30" brace from the table legs to the skirt of the table, so the legs won't fold under unexpectedly, spilling all your goodies all over the ground.

The leg brace (**FIGURE 4**) is made by drilling a hole that will fit loosely on the screw, in one end of a 1" x 2" x 30" board. Cut a narrow notch about 1¼ inches from the opposite end from where you drilled the hole. The top of the leg brace is secured by putting a 1¼" screw into the skirt, and the notch in the brace will slide over the screw in the leg to keep the leg straight (see **FIGURE 5**). Use four braces, two on each set of legs.

After all three tables are made, position them as in **FIGURE 6**. To hold them together, *use C-clamps. You'll need six of the clamps.*

MATERIALS NEEDED FOR UPRIGHTS AND STRINGERS:

Lumber:	10	1" x 4" x 8' (uprights)
	5	1" x 4" x 8' (front, back, middle stringers)
	4	1" x 4" x 10' (side stringers)
	6	C-clamps (not counting the six you've already used)
	20	¼" by 1½" carriage bolts and nuts
	20	¼" washers

Stringers are the upper part of the booth, running horizontally across the top and middle-top.

To add the uprights and stringers, nail two 1" x 4" x 8' uprights together, using more 6d nails, to make a right angle at each corner, as shown at the table corners in **FIGURE 6**. Place the L-shaped uprights in position as shown.

Secure the uprights to the tabletops with C-clamps. You are now ready to bolt the stringers to the uprights. You will use half of them to make the bottom stringer row, and the other half for the top of your booth.

The stringers are to be bolted to the uprights with the carriage bolts and washers, so you will need to drill holes large enough for the carriage bolts in both the uprights and the stringers. Keep in mind that there are two lengths of stringers: the shorter ones will fit across the front and back, and through the middle; the longer ones will be along the sides (see **FIGURE 6**).

After you have attached the lower row of stringers to the uprights *(two feet below the top is a good placement)*, attach the other half of the stringers at the top of your uprights, using the same method – drill holes, use carriage bolts, etc. Using an electric drill speeds up this process considerably, and the drill bit must be large enough to accommodate easy access by the carriage bolts through the holes. **FIGURES 7** and **8** show the front and side views of your booth. **FIGURE 7** shows only the legs of the front table; the legs of the side tables also will be visible to your interested eyes, but for reasons of simplicity, they are not shown in this sketch.

FIGURE 8 shows the legs of one table at the left and approximate middle; the legs at the right of the sketch would belong to the front table.

Your booth is now ready to go. If you feel it needs a bit more support, you may choose to add more hardware. If the spot where it will be set up is level, the above instructions should be more than sufficient.

So – now you're ready to decorate! How you pretty-up your booth will determine how many potential customers are drawn to examine your wares. Be original, which doesn't mean you have to be extravagant, as I've pointed out throughout this book.

You can decorate the booth by covering the area between the two rows of stringers, and by skirting the tables. Bunting is inexpensive and can be used many, many times. Don't forget: the red goes at the bottom!

You can skirt your tables and stringers with commercially purchased cardboard, which comes in long lengths, often in a corrugated finish. Or you can buy some inexpensive cotton fabric at a yardage sale, and use that. Or you may be able to line up a lot of commercial advertising from businesses which would be suitable for use at your booth. If you're serving hot dogs and Coca Cola, you can probably talk the Coke dealer (go to the distributor, not the grocer, for this) out of some bright red corrugated paper or plastic, already decorated with advertising. I'm just using Coke as an example; other firms have similar materials.

You may have items for sale which you can hang from the stringers. If so, use this as part of your overall decorating scheme. The top of our bicentennial watermelon booth was a fanciful, horizontally elongated Uncle Sam's hat. Don't forget to use those resources I've mentioned so often. Get ideas from everyone. At least one will be a winner!

Note: Illustrations are not drawn exactly to scale.

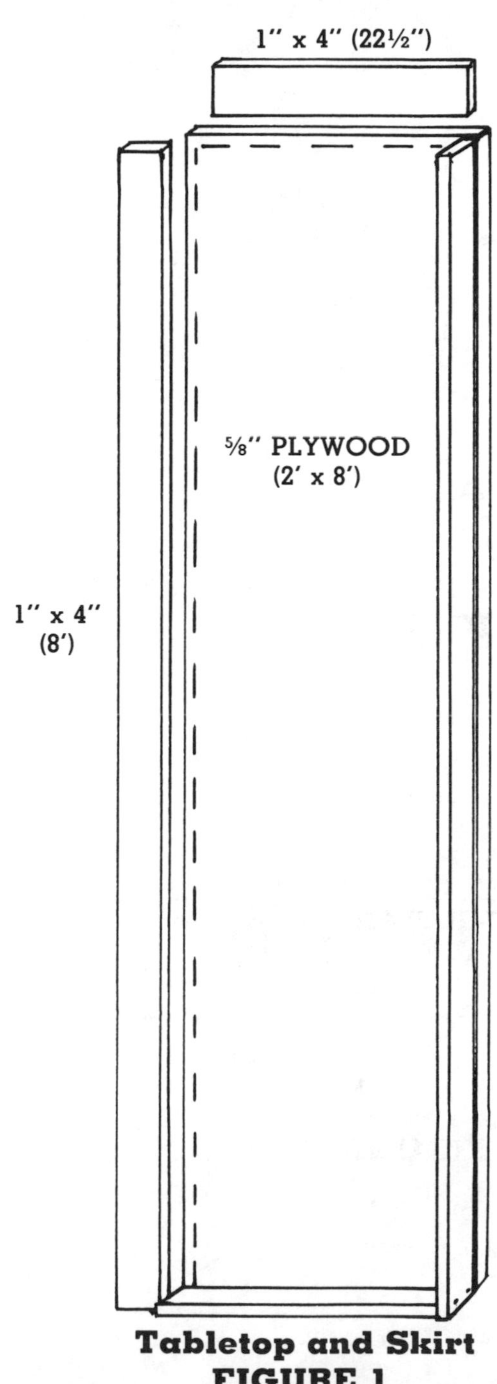

Tabletop and Skirt
FIGURE 1

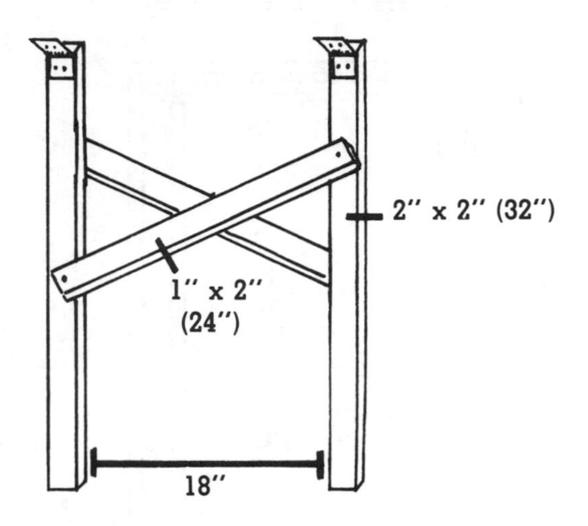

Table Legs and X Brace
FIGURE 2

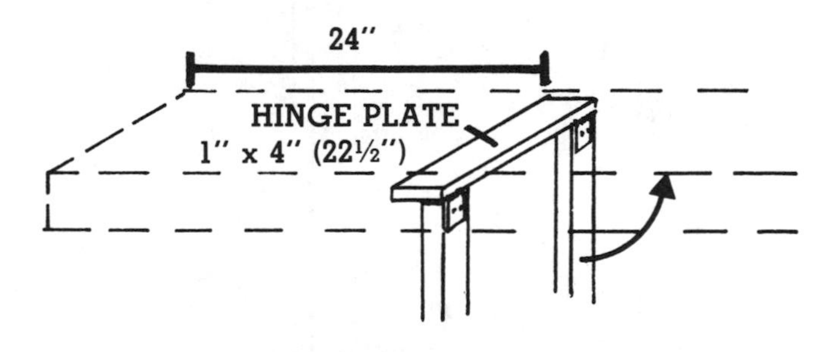

FIGURE 3

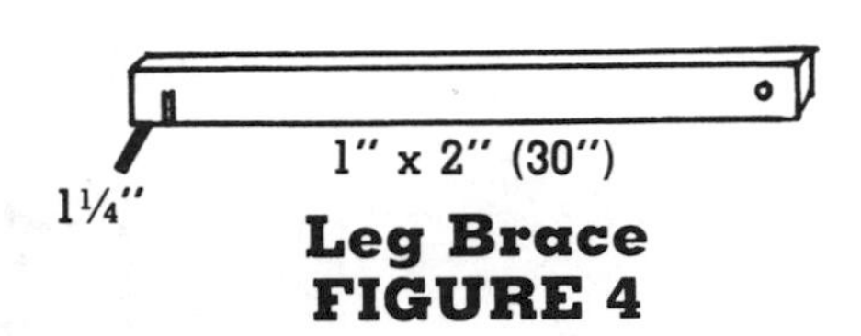

Leg Brace
FIGURE 4

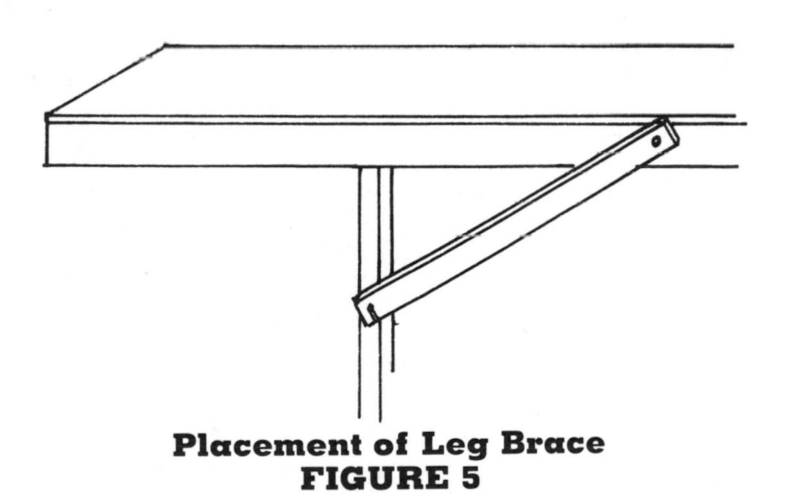

Placement of Leg Brace
FIGURE 5

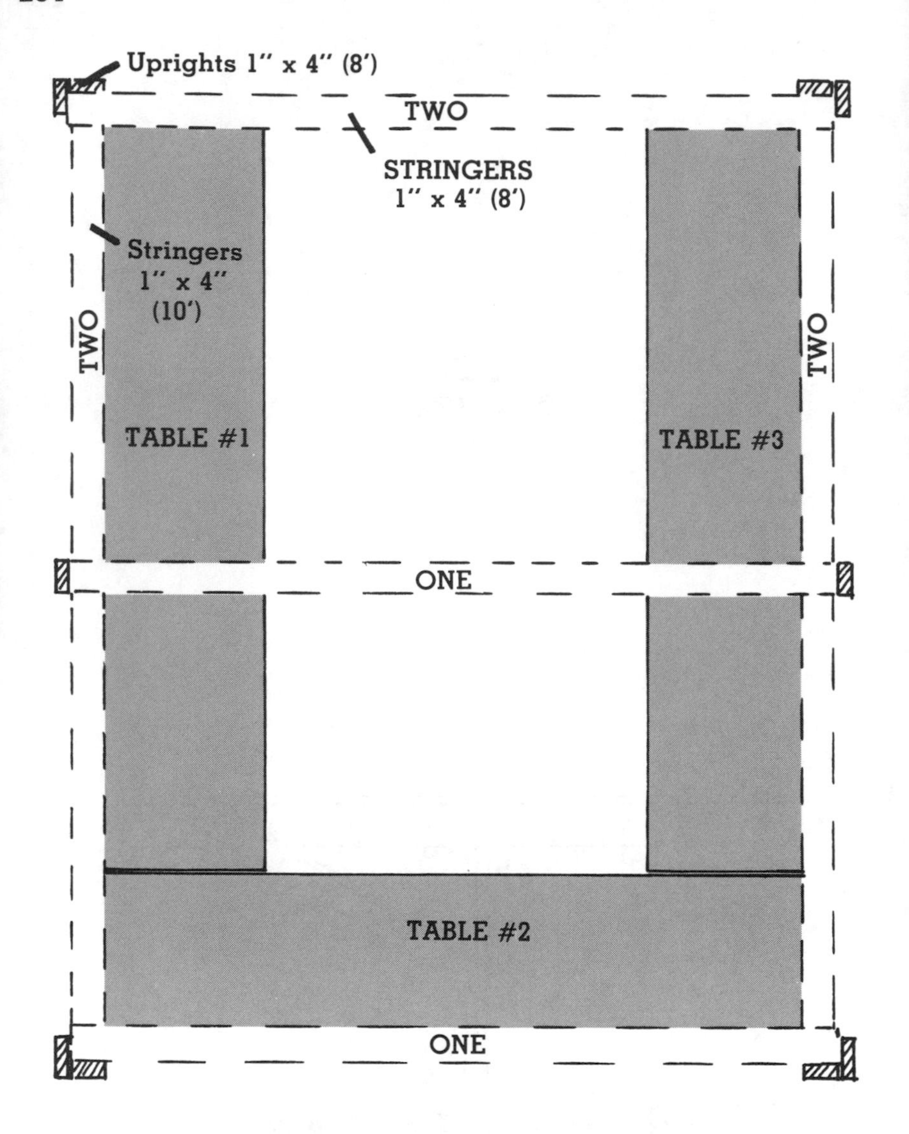

BOOTH
(From Above)

FIGURE 6

NON-DIMENSIONAL FRONT AND SIDE VIEWS OF BOOTH

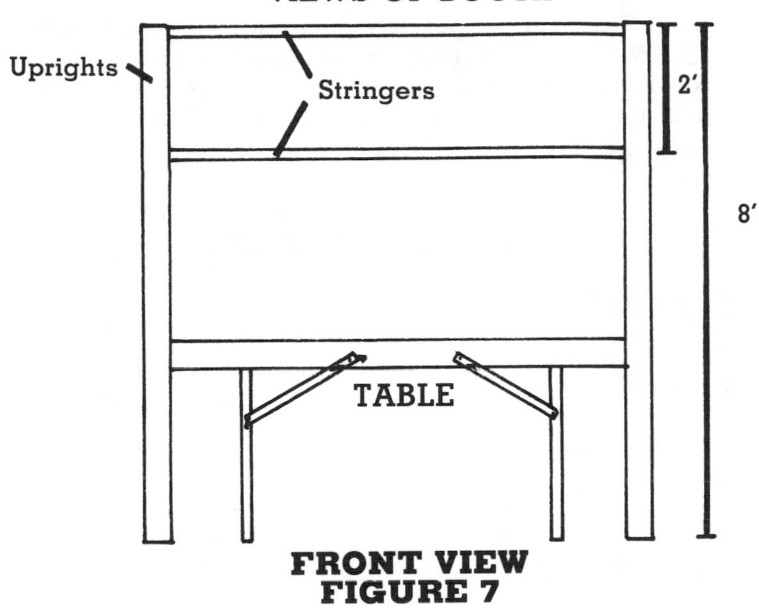

FRONT VIEW
FIGURE 7

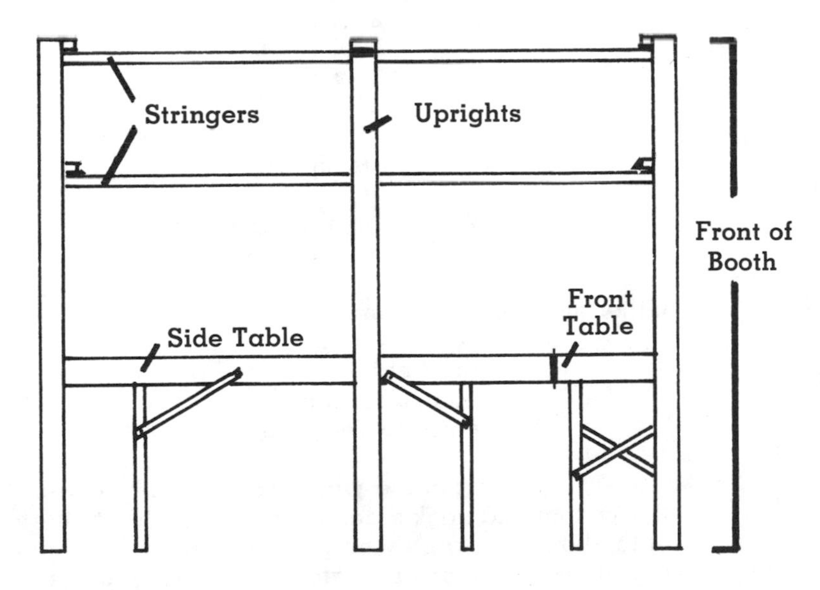

SIDE VIEW
FIGURE 8

The next project is for the construction of a STANDING OVERHEAD SIGN which can be placed over a table or exhibit as wide as seven feet, or placed at the background of an open display. It is over seven feet in height.

MATERIALS NEEDED FOR STANDING SIGN:

Lumber for sign:

2	8" x ½" x 7' plywood pieces
2	8" x 8½" x ½" plywood pieces

Other materials for sign:

4	¼" x 3" bolts and nuts

Lumber for stanchions (or upright legs):

2	2" x 4" x 36"
4	2" x 4" x 6"
2	2" x 4" x 32"
2	2" x 4" x 7'
2	24" x 24" x 34" triangles, as shown
2	16" x 16" x 23" triangles, notched as shown

Other materials for stanchions:

brad nails
bolts and nuts
paint to decorate

The top part of the sign resembles a box with the bottom and back sides missing. The front side of the box is the area where you will put the name of your organization or whatever message you wish to carry out.

Nail the two 7' x 8" x ½" boards together at right angles lengthwise, using brad nails (see **FIGURE A**). Drill holes in the two pieces of 8" x 8½" x ½" wood. Nail one to each end of your L-shaped half-box, closing it at each end. Your results should resemble **FIGURE C**.

Now that you've gotten this far, it's a good time to give your work a first coat of paint. It probably will take at least two coats of paint before you are ready to do the fancy lettering, anyway. By painting the sign top now, you're giving the base paint a chance to dry.

To make the stanchions, nail one 6" x 2" x 4" on each end of the 32" x 2" x 4" as shown in **FIGURE D**. Nail a triangle (the one without a notch in **FIGURE E**) to this so it looks like the lower part of **FIGURE G**. This gives the stanchion stability from side to side.

The triangle with the notch (**FIGURE F**) is then nailed about halfway on the 36" x 2" x 4", as in **FIGURE H**. Leave a space of 1¾" between the 2" x 4" and the notch on the triangle. This gives the stanchion stability from front to back. The two triangular pieces and the upright (7' x 2" x 4") are then nailed together for each side, as in **FIGURE I**.

You are now ready to bolt the L-shaped half-box at the top of the seven-foot uprights (see **FIGURE J**).

After you have bolted the sign portion to the stanchions, you are ready to give the entire standing sign a coat of paint. After the paint is dry, you then will letter the name of your organization across the top (**FIGURE K**), using your logo or any other special design which will make your sign stand out.

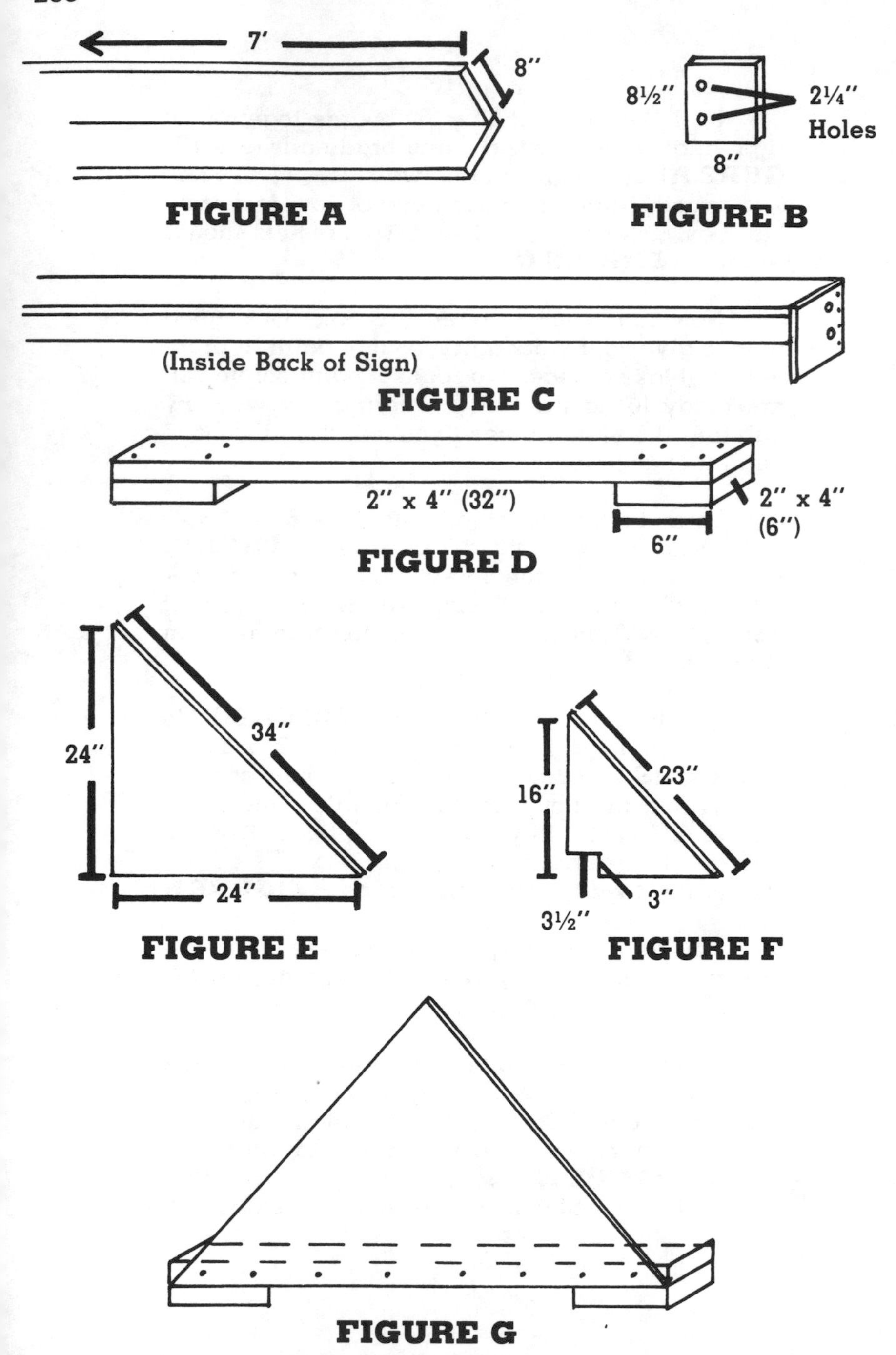

FIGURE A

FIGURE B

FIGURE C

FIGURE D

FIGURE E

FIGURE F

FIGURE G

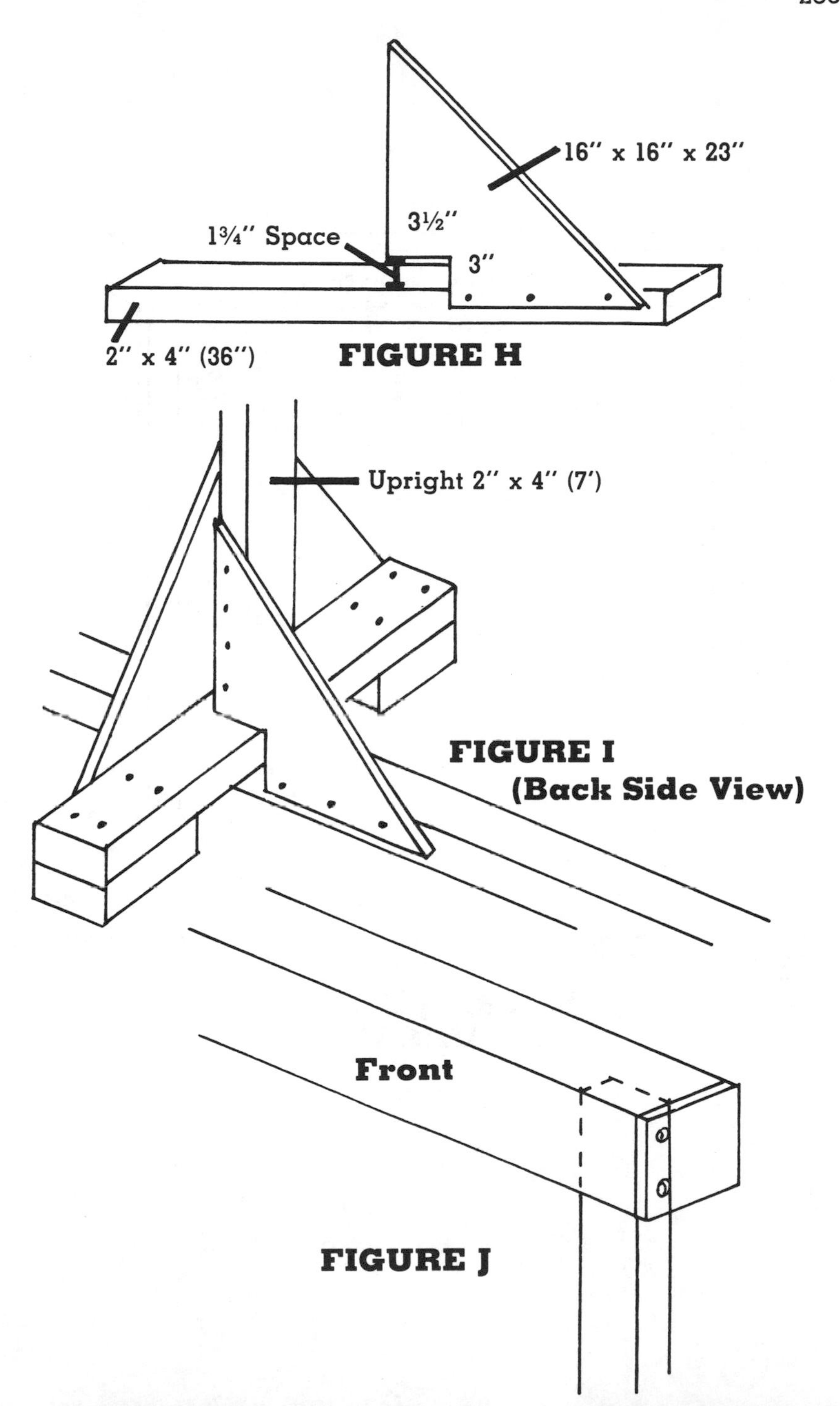

FIGURE H

FIGURE I (Back Side View)

FIGURE J

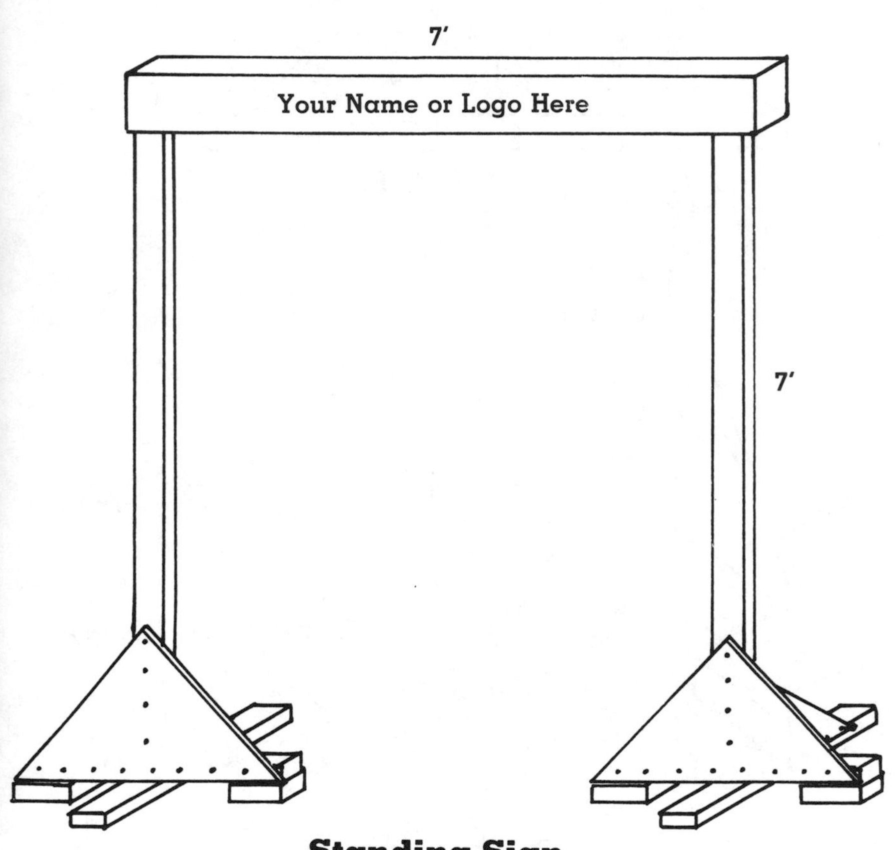

Standing Sign
FIGURE K

So, there you have it – the fun way of raising funds – the way to raise community spirits and community awareness as you work together to raise money for your cause.

If you'll just remember to plan, to use your resources and to know your community, and if you dare to be innovative, there is no reason ever for your club treasury to go dry.

Think of new and exciting ways to spend the money, and then follow through with a rip-roaring fun way of raising the money you intend to spend. May sound like putting the cart before the horse, but it works.

Set your goals – set them high enough to raise some eyebrows – and then prove to the world (not to mention yourself) that it can be done, and that you're the one to do it.

Good luck . . . and . . . have fun!

I did.

ABOUT THE AUTHOR — DORTHY ROSS

After starting her education in a one-room grade school in the vicinity of Pleasant Plains, Illinois, Mrs. Ross' pursuit of excellence continues without pause.

Presently, she writes a weekly column for the *Springfield Herald* and associated newspapers. She also writes a regular youth column for *Illinois Wildlife* and a woman's column for the State Elks Club's *Newsette*.

She is a long-time member of 4-H and has served as a youth leader in this organization for many years. Many other local, state and national youth organizations, from the Rainbow Girls to the Children of the American Revolution, have benefited from her expertise born out of first-hand experience.

To say that Dorthy Ross "has it all together" is an understatement. She's the best kind of authority there is, because what she writes is gospel forged from years of trial and error experience in youth work.

NOTES

NOTES

ORDER FORM

MERIWETHER PUBLISHING LTD.
P.O. BOX 7710
COLORADO SPRINGS, CO 80933
TELEPHONE: (719)594-4422

Please send me the following books:

______**Fund Raising for Youth** **$8.95**
by Dorthy M. Ross #FF-B184
Hundreds of wonderful ways of raising funds for youth organizations

______**Costuming the Christmas and Easter Play** **$5.95**
by Alice M. Staeheli #FF-B180
How to costume any religious play

______**The Complete Banner Handbook** **$10.95**
by Janet Litherland #FF-B172
A complete guide to banner design and construction

______**The Official Sunday School Teachers Handbook** **$7.95**
by Joanne Owens #FF-B152
An indispensable aid and barrel of laughs for anyone involved in Sunday school activities

______**Something for the Kids** **$6.95**
by Ted Lazicki #FF-B192
Fifty-two "front row" sermons for children

______**The Idea Book** **$8.95**
by Rosemary Wesley Hines #FF-B143
A sourcebook of activities for children

______**Clown Act Omnibus** **$9.95**
by Wes McVicar #FF-B118
Everything you want to know about clowning

I understand that I may return any book for a full refund if not satisfied.

NAME: ______________________________

ORGANIZATION NAME: ______________________________

ADDRESS: ______________________________

CITY: ______________________________

PHONE: ______________________________

☐ **Check Enclosed**
☐ **Visa or Master Card #**______________________________

Signature: ______________________________
(required for Visa/Mastercard orders)

COLORADO RESIDENTS: Please add 3% sales tax.

SHIPPING: Include $1.50 for the first book and 50¢ for each additional book ordered.

☐ *Please send me a copy of your complete catalog of books or plays.*